# URUGUAY
## in Pictures

VGS

Alison Behnke

Twenty-First Century Books

# Contents

Twenty-First Century Books
A division of Lerner Publishing Group, Inc.
241 First Avenue North
Minneapolis, MN 55401 U.S.A.

Website address: www.lernerbooks.com

web enhanced @ www.vgsbooks.com

Library of Congress Cataloging-in-Publication Data

Behnke, Alison.
    Uruguay in pictures / by Alison Behnke.
       p.  cm. – (Visual geography series)
    Includes bibliographical references and index.
    ISBN 978-1-57505-961-7 (lib. bdg. : alk. paper)
    1. Uruguay–Juvenile literature. I. Title.
F2708.B34 2010
989.5–dc22                          2008038026

Manufactured in the United States of America
1 2 3 4 5 6 – BP – 15 14 13 12 11 10

# INTRODUCTION

Uruguay is a small nation in southeastern South America. Outsiders often overlook Uruguay. Its large and powerful neighbors, Argentina and Brazil, can overshadow this little nation. But its land is rich in agricultural bounty, with rolling pastures that support cattle, sheep, and crops. And its 3.3 million people—inspired in part by the nation's early heroes, the gauchos (South American cowboys)—are proud of their spirit of self-reliance and independence.

Uruguay was once home to indigenous (native) people called the Charrúa, who lived there thousands of years ago. In the early 1500s, European explorers and colonists began arriving in South America—part of what Europeans called the New World. In the 1600s, Spanish religious workers called missionaries began trying to convert Uruguay's people to Christianity.

Spanish settlers founded Uruguay's capital city of Montevideo in 1726. Within fifty years, the area officially became a Spanish colony. After another half century as a colonial territory, Uruguay

achieved independence in 1828. It enacted its first constitution two years later.

Fairly early in its history as an independent nation, Uruguay thrived. Its people developed the country's resources on prosperous farms and ranches. Many European immigrants settled in the country, expanding the population and bringing their own talents and experience. With an optimistic spirit and hard work, Uruguayans became one of the most prosperous peoples in the Americas. The nation had enough resources for all its citizens, and the fruits of labor were distributed fairly among the people. Political matters were resolved through a democratic system of government.

But Uruguay has also faced its share of challenges. During the 1930s, a worldwide economic slowdown brought turmoil to the government. For four years, Uruguay's democracy turned into a dictatorship (a system in which a single leader has total control). Even when a new constitution in 1934 restored democracy, the nation still struggled.

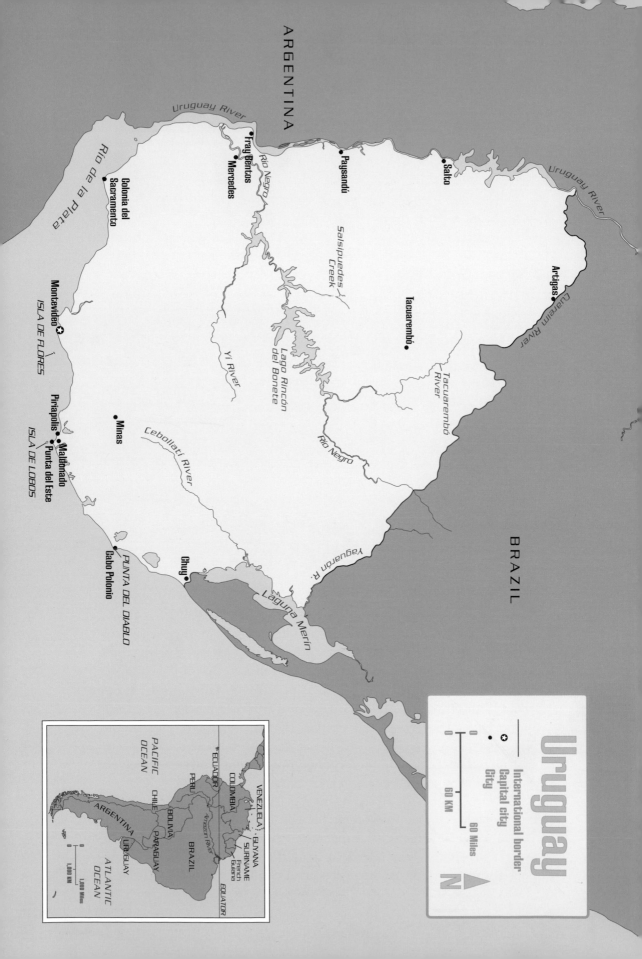

It faced serious financial troubles. The economy declined further in the 1960s, when a terrorist group known as the Tupamaros began staging violent attacks on the government. In response to this violence, Uruguay's armed forces became the country's dominant political force. In 1973, amid increasing turmoil, the military established a dictatorship. Eleven years later, the nation held free, open elections. In 1984 Uruguay's people restored democracy to their nation by electing a president and a congress.

Another economic slowdown in the early 2000s once again brought difficulties. Although conditions improved within a few years, the faltering economy has led many young Uruguayans to seek their fortunes elsewhere. Tens of thousands of Uruguayans have emigrated from the country. Most of them head for Europe or the United States, looking for higher-paying jobs than they can find at home. The country's leaders are eager to slow this trend. They don't want to lose the skills and talents of their bright young citizens.

Through good times and bad, the nation and its people have continued to draw on their gaucho roots and their independent history. They have kept going during the rough patches, and they look forward to an even brighter future.

# The Land

Uruguay covers 68,037 square miles (176,215 square kilometers). It is the second smallest nation of South America, after Suriname. Uruguay is similar in size to the U.S. state of Oklahoma. At its greatest width, from the northwestern corner to the southeastern edge, the country measures fewer than 350 miles (563 km).

Uruguay's formal name is the Eastern Republic of Uruguay, because it lies on the eastern bank of the Uruguay River. This river forms the country's western boundary with Argentina. This river then empties into the broad Río de la Plata. This estuary—a body of water where fresh and salt waters mingle—makes up part of Uruguay's southern boundary. The estuary blends into the South Atlantic Ocean, which borders the country to the southeast. Brazil lies to Uruguay's north and northeast.

## ▶ Topography

Uruguay's topography, or landscape, consists of three main regions. The Western Lowlands stretch along the border with Argentina.

Eastward is the Central Plateau, in the nation's interior. And the Coastal Plain lies along the southern and southeastern coasts.

Uruguay's Western Lowlands form a fertile, level strip of land. Cattle and sheep graze on some of this flat region's grassy plains.

From the Western Lowlands, the terrain rises slightly toward the Central Plateau. Fertile and gently rolling grasslands dominate this part of Uruguay's landscape. The region holds fertile farmland and many prosperous cattle pastures. The area produces meat and wool—the nation's two most important products.

Two hilly ridges interrupt the sweep of the Central Plateau. Called *cuchillas*, these granite formations stick up like blades of knives. The Cuchilla de Haedo lies in the northwest. The Cuchilla Grande extends northeastward toward the Brazilian border. These ridges feature some rugged crests, but they rarely reach elevations of much more than 1,650 feet (503 meters). The nation's highest point is Cerro Catedral, near the southeastern end of the Cuchilla Grande.

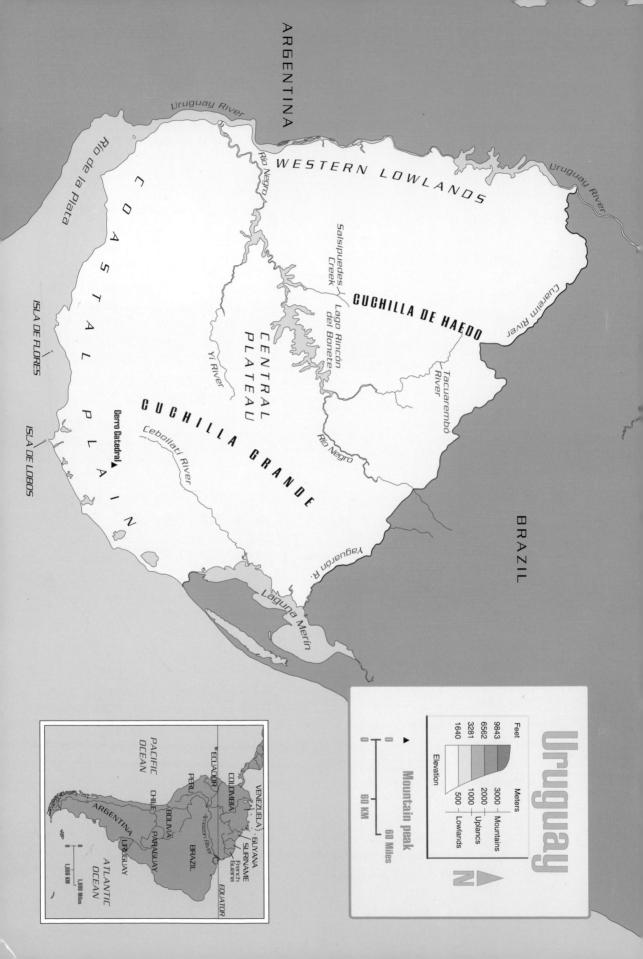

ARGENTINA

*Uruguay River*

*Río de la Plata*

*Río Negro*

WESTERN LOWLANDS

*Uruguay River*

*Salsipuedes Creek*

*Lago Rincón del Bonete*

CUCHILLA DE HAEDO

*Cuaréim River*

ISLA DE FLORES

ISLA DE LOBOS

C O A S T A L   P L A I N

*Yí River*

C E N T R A L   P L A T E A U

*Tacuarembó River*

Cerro Catedral ▲

CUCHILLA GRANDE

*Cebollatí River*

*Río Negro*

*Yaguarón R.*

BRAZIL

Laguna Merín

PACIFIC OCEAN

ECUADOR

COLOMBIA

PERU

CHILE

BOLIVIA

ARGENTINA

PARAGUAY

BRAZIL

URUGUAY

VENEZUELA

*Amazon River*

GUYANA

SURINAME

French Guiana

EQUATOR

ATLANTIC OCEAN

1,000 KM

1,000 Miles

## Uruguay

▲ Mountain peak

Elevation

| Feet | Meters | |
|------|--------|---|
| 9843 | 3000 | Mountains |
| 6562 | 2000 | |
| 3281 | 1000 | Uplands |
| 1640 | 500 | |
| 0 | 0 | Lowlands |

0    60 KM

0    60 Miles

N

This peak rises 1,686 feet (514 m) above sea level.

Uruguay's Coastal Plain lies to the south and east of the Central Plateau. This wide strip of land extends eastward from the capital city of Montevideo in south central Uruguay to the southeastern city of Maldonado and northward to the Brazilian border. This area is the most heavily settled part of Uruguay. Many beaches, lagoons (lakes that are often coastal and may hold saltwater), and windswept sand dunes mark this region.

Uruguay's territory also includes small islands. Numerous islands lie in the Río de la Plata and in the Uruguay River. Others dot the Atlantic Ocean off Uruguay's southern and eastern coasts.

## Rivers, Lakes, and Lagoons

Uruguay's many rivers are important to its economy and environment. For example, they provide access to the sea for Uruguay's exports. They also carry away surplus water from the nation's productive grass lands. Along their riverbanks, narrow ribbons of forest crisscross the country.

The Río Negro is the nation's largest inland waterway. Its name means "Black River" in Spanish and comes from its clear, dark waters. From its source in Brazil, the Río Negro flows to the southwest, dividing Uruguay roughly in half. It is deep enough for ships to sail about 45 miles (72 km) inland from the Río de la Plata. Lowlands along the Río Negro widen into a large area of forest as the river joins the Uruguay River.

The Río Negro's tributaries (rivers that flow into other rivers) include the Tacuarembó River. It flows southward from near the Brazilian border and meets the Río Negro in central Uruguay. Another tributary is the Yi River, which rises in the Cuchilla Grande. Its course runs for about 140 miles (225 km) before flowing into the Río Negro.

Other rivers and streams, such as the Cebollatí River, also begin in the Cuchilla Grande. These waterways run eastward along shallow courses. They eventually feed either into lagoons near the Atlantic coast or directly into the ocean.

The lighthouse at Cabo Polonio was built in 1880.

Many major waterways run along Uruguay's borders. The nation's frontier with Brazil includes the Cuareim and Yaguarón rivers. The Río de la Plata borders southwestern Uruguay for more than 150 miles (241 km). This estuary and its tributaries carry surplus water away from about one-third of South America's land. The Río de la Plata is also very important to Uruguayan trade and business. Oceangoing vessels navigate the river to unload their cargoes at the port of Montevideo. And the Uruguay River, from which the country takes its name, actually rises in Brazil. It flows southward to the Río de la Plata, tracing Uruguay's western border as it goes.

A few large—but artificial—lakes lie in central Uruguay. The 87-mile-long (140 km) Lago Rincón del Bonete (also known as Embalse del Río Negro) formed as the result of a dam on the Río Negro. In the 1940s, engineers built the dam to create hydroelectric power (energy created by rushing water).

Freshwater and saltwater lagoons lie along Uruguay's Atlantic coast. One of the largest is Laguna Merín, in eastern Uruguay. The country shares this shallow body of water, which holds both salt- and freshwater,

Central Uruguay's Lago Rincón del Bonete is the largest artificial lake in South America. It covers approximately 4,000 square miles (10,360 sq. km).

with Brazil. (In Brazil, it is called Mirim Lagoon.) Many smaller lagoons also dot the coast.

## Climate

Uruguay's climate is mild. Temperatures do not vary widely. About one-third of each year's days are sunny. Humidity is often high, especially during the winter months of July and August.

Because Uruguay is in the Southern Hemisphere (south of the equator, the line around the center of Earth), its seasons are the opposite of those in the Northern Hemisphere. So winter lasts from about June through September. Summer begins in about December and ends in March.

Winter temperatures range from about 50°F to 60°F (10°C to 16°C). While temperatures sometimes drop to freezing (32°F, or 0°C), it rarely snows. But winds from the ocean often make it feel quite cold. Summer temperatures average between 70°F and 81°F (21°C and 27°C). Uruguay's summer weather, however, often changes unpredictably. Looming clouds and cold southern winds may suddenly interrupt a warm, sunny afternoon with a sharp drop in temperature.

Winter is the rainiest season, but heavy storms occur in the autumn. Summer thunderstorms are also common. In the south, Montevideo receives about 37 to 45 inches (94 to 114 centimeters) of rainfall a year. Approximately 50 to 55 inches (127 to 140 cm) of rain fall in the north, while the nation's center is slightly drier. Uruguay sometimes experiences severe shortages of rain called droughts. Drought struck the nation in 2008 and 2009.

Visit www.vgsbooks.com for links to websites with additional information about land features and weather conditions in Uruguay.

## Flora and Fauna

In the springtime, colorful wildflowers cover Uruguay's rural landscape. The purple and white flowers of verbena often give a lavender hue to grasslands. Pink mimosa, deep red ceibo, and white myrtle blossoms also brighten the country.

Forests cover less than 10 percent of Uruguay's land. Forest growth is thickest in the far northwest and along riverbanks. Trees native to the country include the willow, acacia, myrtle, and laurel. Lignum vitae is a valuable hardwood, and the quebracho's bark is used in tanning (preparing) leather. In southeastern Uruguay, a belt of tropical palm trees stretches across the country. Some historians believe this line marks a trade route dating back to the 1400s or earlier.

Another native tree is the thick-trunked ombú. It often appears in paintings and drawings of Uruguay. A single tree often has several large trunks. Its wood is too soft to be useful for building or as fuel. But the ombú's wide canopy of leaves provides welcome shade in Uruguay's sunny plains.

People have also brought nonnative trees to Uruguay. Eucalyptus trees from Australia dot the land, and poplars line many roadways. Pines planted behind the Atlantic beaches help stabilize the soil and prevent sand dunes from creeping inland. Growers have also introduced a wide range of fruit and nut trees. These include peach, pear, lemon, olive, almond, and date trees.

Pumas (mountain lions), jaguars, and other wildcats once roamed Uruguay. But hunters drove most of these mammals into extinction long ago. However, nature lovers can still spot deer, fox, and the capybara—the world's largest rodent. The mulita, a small armadillo, survives in the northern hills. The nutria, a rodent with beaverlike fur, swims in Uruguay's rivers. Seals live on the Isla de Lobos, a rocky island off the southern Atlantic coast. The island boasts one of the globe's most important seal-breeding grounds. Uruguayan authorities strictly control and protect this wildlife sanctuary.

**South American sea lions** lounge on the rocky coast of Uruguay. These sea lions are found along the South American coast.

Reptiles in Uruguay include caimans (semiaquatic reptiles similar to alligators), a variety of lizards, and snakes such as the poisonous South American rattlesnake. The nation is also home to tortoises and sea turtles.

Uruguay's birdlife is rich and varied. Flightless Antarctic penguins swim northward to Uruguayan beaches. Another flightless bird, the rhea, or South American ostrich, runs across Uruguay's open plains with giant strides. The southern burrowing owl is about the size of a robin. Unlike most owls, it is active during the day.

Ocean birds such as terns are plentiful. Wading birds, including snipes, stalk the beaches looking for food. Inland, parakeets are common, and partridges and prairie hens live in the interior's open pastures. Horneros—also called oven-birds—use mud to build round nests on the top of fence posts and telephone poles. The crow-sized *teruterú*, whose name comes from its cry, has dramatic black-and-white bands and a sharp spur on the edge of each wing.

The waters off Uruguay's southeastern coast hold many fish. Species here include black bass, mackerel, tuna, bluefish, anchovy, mullet, sole, piranhas, and drum—so called because it makes a drumming noise. Uruguay's rivers are home to the dorado. This salmonlike fish averages 30 pounds (14 kilograms) but may weigh up to 60 pounds (27 kg).

The **rhea** can grow to 5.6 feet (1.7 m) tall.

## ▶ Natural Resources and Environmental Challenges

Uruguay's greatest natural resource is its pastureland. Farmers use nearly 80 percent of the nation for growing crops or for raising sheep and cattle. The country's many rivers are also valuable resources, producing large amounts of hydroelectric power and providing transportation routes.

Beyond these assets, Uruguay has few natural resources. The lack of large amounts of energy sources such as coal or oil has held back industrial development. The country does hold manganese, copper, lead, gold, and iron, but only in small amounts. The nation is also home to marble quarries. Marble is a beautiful stone with many colors and textures. Builders in Uruguay and beyond use it in construction. In addition, many artists like to use marble for sculpture. Uruguay also exports some granite, limestone, talc, and sand.

The nation faces several environmental issues. Waste from industries such as leather tanning and meatpacking pollutes Uruguay's rivers. Industrial air pollution and waste disposal are also problems. And in 2008, two ships crashed off Uruguay's coast on the Río de la Plata. The resulting oil spill killed more than fifty penguins, as well as threatening other wildlife. In addition, some of Uruguay's animals are endangered because their wildlife habitat is becoming farmland or grazing land.

A gaucho (cowboy) leads **cattle** to graze. The broad pastures of Uruguay are ideal for raising animals, such as cattle and sheep, that feed on nutritious grasses.

The nation's government has taken steps to address these issues. For example, Uruguayan leaders have signed international treaties pledging to protect the environment. And national parks in the country provide shelter for plant and animal life. But environmental concerns remain.

## ◉ Cities and Towns

Uruguay has few big cities. By far its largest urban center is the capital, Montevideo. The country also has a few major towns, as well as many small villages.

MONTEVIDEO is home to more than 1.3 million people—more than one-third of Uruguay's entire population. Spanish settlers founded the city in 1726. It soon became Uruguay's chief seaport. It was also a center of colonial government and of defense against other colonial powers, especially the Portuguese. The capital grew into a lively commercial town, with shopkeepers, merchants, lawyers, and doctors.

The present-day capital remains the hub of the country's government, business, and culture. Interesting old buildings stand alongside modern high-rises. In the old port district, narrow streets hold fine colonial-era houses. The Mercado del Puerto (Port Market)

Montevideo is a bustling, modern city. This view is of **the Rambla,** the street in Montevideo that runs along the coast.

## WHAT'S IN A NAME?

In the early 1500s, a Portuguese explorer named Ferdinand Magellan sailed from Europe to South America's eastern coast. According to legend, when one of Magellan's lookouts saw the site of Uruguay's future capital, he cried out, "*Monte vide eu!*" These words, meaning "I see a mountain!" in Portuguese, gave Montevideo its name.

also stands in this neighborhood. This huge iron-framed building was once a train station. It holds shops and stands selling everything from cheese and grilled meats to books and clothes. Montevideo also has many museums, as well as attractive parks and open spaces.

SALTO is the country's second-largest city, with close to 100,000 residents. It is a port city on the Uruguay River, lying in northwestern Uruguay.

Another important port on the Uruguay River is PAYSANDÚ, with a population of about 80,000. It lies

Uruguay's beautiful coastal cities, such as **Piriapolis,** attract tourists from other South American countries.

approximately 65 miles (105 km) south of Salto and is an industrial city with many factories.

Other towns of note include Maldonado and Fray Bentos. Maldonado is a colonial-era town on the Atlantic coast that was once a pirate stronghold. In modern times, it has a population of about 55,000. Fray Bentos is a meatpacking hub on the Uruguay River and is home to about 23,000 people. Punta del Este is the country's leading resort area. Located on the Atlantic coast, east of Montevideo, it has only about 15,000 permanent residents. But during the summertime, its beautiful beaches and luxurious hotels can draw between 500,000 and 1 million tourists. Most of these visitors come from Argentina. Punta del Este also serves as a conference site for international meetings.

Uruguay's rural towns and villages tend to be quiet places surrounded by outlying ranches and farms. Many towns are located on well-paved roads that fan out from the capital. These routes carry the countryside's agricultural exports to Montevideo. From there, ships take them all around the continent and beyond.

# HISTORY AND GOVERNMENT

Humans began settling in South America as early as 10,000 to 15,000 B.C. They came to the region from the north. Even earlier, people had migrated from Siberia (part of modern-day Russia) to Alaska across a land bridge that once connected these areas. Gradually, human settlement spread southward.

In the area that became Uruguay, the largest group of indigenous people was the Charrúa. The Charrúa lived in small villages made up of about ten families. They moved their homes around the region according to the season. During summer's warm months, they lived along the Atlantic coast and the Río de la Plata. They fished in these productive waters. They also gathered fruit and other natural foods in the area. During the cooler parts of the year, they traveled to Uruguay's interior and hunted animals for their food. The Charrúa were fierce warriors and sometimes battled neighboring groups over disagreements. Their weapons included bows and arrows, as well as clubs.

## ○ Early Explorers

During the late fifteenth and early sixteenth century, European explorers began venturing across the Atlantic Ocean to the Americas. They called these lands the New World. The Italian explorer Christopher Columbus arrived in the New World in 1492. He first landed among islands in the Caribbean Sea. Columbus's expedition was on behalf of Spain, and Spanish adventurers and settlers soon followed. Some of them arrived in what would later be Uruguay.

In 1516 the Spanish explorer Juan Díaz de Solís sailed up the Río de la Plata and dropped anchor near the future site of Montevideo. He was looking along the Río de la Plata for a water passage through South America to the Pacific Ocean. But when Díaz de Solís and his men went ashore, a local Charrúa group launched an attack. They killed Díaz de Solís and most of his party.

The next major explorer to arrive was Ferdinand Magellan. Magellan was a Portuguese captain in the service of Spain. He was the first person to lead an expedition to sail around the world. In 1520 he traveled along the southern coast of Uruguay. Like Díaz de Solís, he was looking for a passage to the Pacific. Seven years later, the English sailor Sebastian Cabot (exploring on behalf of Spain) reached the Uruguayan coast. During this visit, Cabot gave the Río de la Plata its name, which means "River of Silver." The explorer may have been inspired by the water's shimmering surface. Or perhaps he mistakenly thought that the river's banks were rich in silver deposits. No one knows for certain.

## Cowboys and Missionaries

During this period, Europeans—especially from Spain and Portugal— were settling much of South America. They formed colonies and claimed territory on behalf of their rulers back in Europe. But during the rest of the 1500s, none of these explorers and colonists founded major settlements in Uruguay. A major reason for their focus else- where was that Uruguay did not have large amounts of gold, silver, or other precious resources. The region's native inhabitants continued to follow their traditional way of life with little outside interruption.

The following century, however, brought new activity with the arrival of cattle ranchers and Christian missionaries (religious work- ers). The ranchers arrived first. Most historians credit a man named Hernando Arias de Saavedra with introducing ranching to Uruguay. Arias became the first governor of Spain's territory in the Río de la Plata area. The region included the city of Buenos Aires (in present-day Argentina) and much of the surrounding area. In the early 1600s, Arias decided that Uruguay's lush green pastures would be a perfect place for raising livestock. He brought several dozen cattle and horses to Uruguay from Argentina and turned them loose. The herds thrived and grew quickly on the abundant grass- lands. Soon the large number of untamed cattle and horses attracted the attention of gauchos, or cow- boys. These gauchos lived across the Río de la Plata in a well-settled area around Buenos Aires.

The rugged gauchos were inde- pendent individuals with no perma- nent homes. They cared little about land ownership or about developing

### TOOLS OF THE TRADE

One of the Charrúa's weapons was the bola. It consisted of stones or balls on the ends of leather cords. Bolas were good for hunting as well as fighting. When a person threw a bola, its cord could tangle up in a target's legs, while the stones could sometimes knock the prey unconscious. Later, gauchos adopted this ancient tool and used it to rope horses and cows.

This painting shows a gaucho hunting a rhea. The gaucho is about to throw a bola, a tool gauchos borrowed from the Charrúa.

settled communities. They preferred simply to follow the cattle herds, relying on the animals' meat for food and their skins for clothing. Gauchos eventually became heroic figures in the literature and folklore of the area.

In 1624 religious missionaries began coming to Uruguay. They intended to convert the Charrúa people to their own religion of Roman Catholicism. Catholicism is a branch of Christianity and was Spain's official religion at the time. Most of these Catholic missionaries were Jesuits, members of a specific order of Catholicism. In Uruguay and other parts of the region, the Jesuits tried to make the Charrúa and other indigenous peoples adopt European ways and culture as well as Christianity. However, the Charrúa resisted the Jesuits' efforts and tried to maintain their traditional way of life.

## Rivalry with Portugal

Meanwhile, Uruguay had become part of a rivalry between Spain and Portugal. Both nations wanted to control as much of South America as they could. They were founding colonies around the continent. This intense rivalry for territory and trade began within the region of the Río de la Plata. In defiance of Spanish claims, the Portuguese established a settlement in 1680 at Colonia del Sacramento. This town was in Uruguayan territory, across the Río de la Plata from Spain's settlement at Buenos Aires.

Colonia threatened Spain's control over the Río de la Plata. The river was a vital route for Spain's valuable export of South American goods. To counter the challenge, Spanish troops swiftly captured and occupied the town. The incident sparked a feud between Spain and Portugal that lasted for the next century and a half.

While Portugal posed an ongoing threat, most of Uruguay was in Spanish hands by the early 1700s. In 1726 Spanish settlers founded Montevideo. It began primarily as a military fort to guard against Portuguese threats. Over time it grew into a thriving city with a busy port, businesses, and a town council called a *cabildo*.

This development and colonization came at a great cost to Uruguay's indigenous population. Spanish and Portuguese colonists killed or drove out many of the native Charrúa people. European diseases also killed some Charrúa, who had never been exposed to these illnesses. Other indigenous people intermarried with Europeans. Soon, very few full-blooded Charrúa remained.

Another human cost came in the form of slavery. In the mid-1700s, colonists in South America began bringing people taken from Africa to do hard, unpaid labor in the growing colonies. Most slaves in Uruguay worked on cattle ranches.

Spain's rivalry with Portugal soon cropped up again. In 1763 Portugal regained control of Colonia and held it for more than a decade. Meanwhile, Spain still worked to prevent other challenges to its control. Spanish rulers had grown worried about the power of the Catholic Church. Many of the missionaries and church officials in the region had become very wealthy and influential. So in 1767, the Spanish crown expelled the Jesuit priests from Uruguay. Several years later, Spain finally took permanent possession of Colonia. Spain had also by this time strengthened its grip over the rest of Uruguay's territory and beyond.

## Viceroyalty of the Río de la Plata

In 1776 Spain's rulers created the Viceroyalty of the Río de la Plata. A viceroyalty is a territory governed by an official who acts on behalf of a colonizing nation's ruler. The new viceroyalty's headquarters were in Buenos Aires. In addition to the present-day territory of Argentina, the viceroyalty included the area of modern Paraguay and Uruguay and parts of Bolivia, Brazil, and Chile.

The small colony of Uruguay and its capital of Montevideo had a low status in this new arrangement. Most Uruguayans resented the change. Their resentment smoldered for the next two decades.

Near the end of the eighteenth century, Spain and Britain were at war. As time went by, the British began to take the upper hand.

The conflict moved to the New World when the British occupied Buenos Aires in 1807. They took over Montevideo in 1808. That same year, the French commander Napoléon Bonaparte and his armies overran Spain. They imprisoned Spain's king, Ferdinand VII, and placed Napoléon's brother Joseph on the Spanish throne. Settlers in Uruguay and elsewhere in South America were divided in their loyalties. Some pledged their allegiance to Ferdinand, while others supported Joseph Bonaparte.

## José Artigas

Uruguayans were angry about Britain's presence in Montevideo. And they still felt that the far-off authorities in Spain were doing a poor job of running their homeland. Soon they began to talk about independence for Uruguay. One leader of this growing independence movement was José Gervasio Artigas Arnal.

Artigas came from a Montevideo family, but he had adopted the gaucho way of life. Like many other Uruguayans, he was concerned about the future of his country. Determined to fight for his nation's independence, he organized an army of gaucho forces. In 1811 he led these forces in attacking Montevideo, the seat of Spanish rule in Uruguay. Portuguese troops from Brazil intervened, hoping to seize Uruguay for themselves. In response,

This painting of **General José Artigas** is on display in the Buenos Aires National History Museum.

Artigas led about 15,000 Uruguayans—one-fourth of the total population—to the Uruguay River's west bank in neighboring Argentina and beyond to Paraguay.

For two years, Artigas refused to submit to the Spanish authorities in Buenos Aires. He demanded a guarantee of complete autonomy (self-rule) for Uruguay. Buenos Aires rejected the demand in 1813, and the next year Buenos Aires troops captured Montevideo. But Artigas and his gauchos drove them out in 1815 and declared independence.

Artigas and the rebels set up a government patterned after the United States. For a time, they managed to hold a large territory. It included not only the eastern bank of the Río de la Plata (then called the Banda Oriental) but also the northern provinces of Argentina.

But in 1816, a new, larger, and stronger Portuguese force from Brazil got involved again. Portugal still hoped to take control of Uruguay. The Spanish in Buenos Aires opposed this plan, but Portuguese forces still drove Artigas out of Uruguay. He withdrew to Argentina's northern provinces. From there, he continued to oppose both Spanish and Portuguese armies. When Portuguese forces took control of Montevideo and finally defeated him in 1820, Artigas fled to Paraguay. He lived in poverty there for thirty years. Nevertheless, Artigas remains a Uruguayan hero. His admirers say that his deeds created a Uruguayan sense of national pride and laid the foundations of the country's future independence.

## The Thirty-Three Immortals

Before Artigas could complete his mission, the Portuguese in Brazil took control of the Banda Oriental. Brazilian rule was mild, but the Uruguayans' newfound pride suffered. In 1825 a group of Uruguayan exiles living in Argentina invaded their homeland to free it.

Juan Antonio Lavalleja and José Fructuoso Rivera led these rebels, who became known as the Thirty-Three Immortals. The group quickly gained the support of the local population. In addition, Spanish authorities in Buenos Aires saw the revolt as a chance to gain influence over the Banda Oriental themselves. They sent forces on land and sea to help the rebels.

Argentine intervention brought war between Argentina and Brazil. The Brazilians blockaded Buenos Aires, sealing off its port and blocking traffic in or out. The blockade nearly halted Britain's trade in the area. Eager to resume the profitable business, British officials negotiated a settlement between Argentina and Brazil in 1828. To the joy of Uruguayans, the settlement finally made their country independent. Britain's leaders hoped that this independent state would act as a buffer between Argentina and Brazil.

## Nationhood

At the time of independence, Uruguay's future did not seem very promising. The land was sparsely populated, with fewer than 100,000 people. Most were either gauchos or shepherds and their families. Only in the capital city was there a group of people with more than a very basic education. This elite group took on the task of creating a government for the new nation.

On July 18, 1830, Uruguay enacted its first constitution. This document would remain in effect for almost ninety years. At that time in South America, such a long-lasting constitution was rare. One probable reason for the Uruguayan constitution's survival was the freedom that it allowed. For example, Uruguay's leaders fiercely protected free speech within the nation's parliament (legislature, or law-making branch) even when legislators voiced views that directly opposed those of the president.

These measures did not mean that Uruguay's early decades were easy or calm, however. Not everyone benefited equally from the new system. For example, women could not vote. And in addition to threats from its much larger neighbors, the young nation suffered from internal strife. The new constitution had made José Fructuoso Rivera the country's first president.

But Fructuoso had a political rival. Manuel Oribe had fought alongside Fructuoso as one of the Thirty-Three Immortals. When Oribe became president in 1834, Fructuoso revolted against him.

By the mid-1830s, two well-defined—and fiercely opposed—political parties had emerged from these internal struggles. Manuel Oribe headed a group called the Blancos, or Whites, because of the white ribbons they wore on their hats. The Blancos mainly represented gauchos,

## A TRAGIC ENDING

The final and most devastating attack on the Charrúa people came in 1831. On April 11 of that year, an armed group of Uruguayan soldiers ambushed most of the remaining Charrúa. The creek where the attack took place came to be known as Salsipuedes—meaning "get out if you can" in Spanish.

The soldiers killed between forty and three hundred Charrúa people in the massacre at Salsipuedes. Only four survived. The soldiers captured these survivors and sold them to a French man who took them to France to display them to curious spectators. But three soon died of illness and starvation. The fourth—a man named Tacuabe—escaped with the baby daughter of one of the other survivors. No one knows what became of them, but a monument in Tacuabe's memory stands in Montevideo.

**Blancos soldiers** in Oribe's army are shown on horses in this 1844 painting.

shepherds, and other rural citizens. José Fructuoso led their opponents, who wore red ribbons and were named the Colorados, or Reds. The Colorados were more supportive of the residents of Montevideo and their business interests. Each group had its own private army. As battles between the groups increased, the rivalry grew into a civil war. Uruguayans call this war the Guerra Grande (Great War).

## THE PRICE OF FREEDOM

The Great War killed many people and took a heavy toll on Uruguay. But it also brought a positive change. During the conflict, both the Blancos and the Colorados abolished slavery. They did this because they wanted former slaves to become soldiers in the war.

## ⊙ Struggles and Strife

The intervention of other nations sometimes complicated Uruguay's Great War. In 1843 the Blancos attacked Montevideo, which the Colorados held at the time. The Argentine dictator Juan Manuel de Rosas supported the Blancos in this effort. Oribe's Blancos, with Argentine help, set up a naval blockade and also attacked the Colorados on land. The siege of Montevideo would last for close to nine years. (A siege is a military operation in which forces surround an area and cut it off from outside supplies and aid.)

In addition to drawing in Argentina and Brazil, the Great War also involved European nations. France and Britain were eager to stabilize South America to protect their own business and trade there. The British sent supplies to the besieged Montevideo, and both France and Britain blockaded Buenos Aires.

These international efforts eventually defeated the Blancos. The Colorados gained control of the country, and in 1851 the parties signed treaties ending the Great War. These peace agreements also made Uruguay an ally of Brazil, which had helped the Colorados achieve victory.

But peace was short-lived in Uruguay. Twice during the next sixteen years, President Venancio Flores of the Colorados requested Brazilian help to keep him in office against Blanco challenges. In return for this help, Flores joined Uruguay with Argentina and Brazil in the War of the Triple Alliance. They fought against heavily armed, but hopelessly overpowered, Paraguay. This war lasted from 1865 to 1870.

**Uruguayans tried to defend the city of Paysandú against Paraguay in a battle in 1865.**

## A Lasting Law

The life of Uruguay's first constitution—from 1830 to 1919—was unusual in South America at the time. Many governments rewrote their early constitutions after just a few years. For example, Ecuador enacted its first constitution in 1830 and rewrote it in 1835. Bolivia's first constitution lasted from 1826 to 1831, while Argentina's initial postindependence constitution was in effect from 1853 to 1860.

No sooner was this conflict over than strife between the Blancos and Colorados once again tore Uruguay apart. The Colorados easily emerged the winners. By 1872 they were strong enough to hold onto power. Widespread acceptance of this fact led both Colorado and Blanco leaders to strike a deal. The Blancos gained control of key public offices and local police forces in four of the country's nine departments (provinces, or states). The Colorados dominated the rest of the departments and ran the national government. Following a brief uprising in 1897, Blanco control was increased to include six departments. This arrangement provided the basic organization of Uruguay's two-party system.

While Uruguay's leaders hammered out their system for exercising national and local power, Uruguay itself was changing. Revolutionary violence ended, and the nation's leaders succeeded each other peacefully. In contrast to the earlier gaucho caudillos (political leaders), more and more of Uruguay's presidents and public officials were army officers.

During the late nineteenth century, heavy immigration from Europe, especially from Italy, added to these social and political changes. The immigrants and their families—many of them skilled workers—made great contributions to Uruguayan life. In addition to expanding the nation's population and productivity, they demanded improvements in the country's schools.

## José Batlle y Ordóñez

As the nation's political situation improved, José Batlle y Ordóñez appeared on the scene. Son of a former Uruguayan president, Batlle was a successful businessman who had founded a leading newspaper. He was also a prominent politician. After several years' service as a congressman, he was elected senator in 1898 and president in 1903.

Batlle had a strong personality, new ideas, and a genius for political organization. He served twice as president, from 1903 to 1907 and from 1911 to 1915. Batlle sought and won support from the nation's workers and middle class—two groups that previous political candidates had often neglected.

Under Batlle's leadership, armed politics gave way to more democratic politics—though not without a fight. The fight was a Blanco rebellion, which lasted nearly a year. It began on December 25, 1903. Government forces defeated the rebels on September 1, 1904. The end of this rebellion, after the long string of conflicts, brought Uruguayans a new sense of purpose and a positive national outlook.

Batlle promoted education, improved conditions for workers, and made government more efficient. During his years in office, his government oversaw the building of railroads, the modernization of ports, and the introduction of waterworks, gas, electricity, and telephones.

In 1914 World War I broke out among several European powers. Uruguay declared that it would remain neutral in the conflict, but it later broke off diplomatic relations with Germany in 1917. However, Uruguay did not take an active role in the war, which ended in 1918.

Meanwhile, Batlle and the government created a new constitution that took effect in 1919. It provided for an elected president and a bicameral (two-house) congress. The document also created a nine-member National Council of Administration, also called the *colegiado*. This council shared power with the president. It included members who were not in the same political party as the president.

## The Mid-Twentieth Century

Following Batlle's principles, the government of Uruguay worked fairly smoothly until the Great Depression. This severe worldwide economic decline lasted from 1929 until the mid-1930s. During these years, the normal workings of government broke down. President Gabriel Terra argued with the National Council of Administration. The congress attempted to impeach him (charge and try him for misconduct in office). After using force to suppress his opposition, Terra dissolved both the council and the congress. For the next four years, he ruled as a dictator. He imprisoned political opponents and suspended the 1919 constitution. In 1934 he put a new constitution into effect. It once again provided for a democratic form of government led by an elected president. And it was the first to guarantee women the right to vote (a right they had officially won two years earlier). But many voters and political opponents still did not trust Terra and feared he would try to hold onto power. Nevertheless, elections took place in 1938, and General Alfredo Baldomir became the new president.

In 1939 world war once again broke out in Europe. At first, Uruguay remained neutral and uninvolved. But in 1942, Baldomir broke off relations with the war's Axis (pro-German) powers. The nation officially

Uruguay stopped using the **Isla de Flores prison** in 1970. Since then, only the lighthouse keepers have lived on the island. But old buildings, including the jailhouse, remain standing.

## AN ISLAND PRISON

During the 1930s, President Gabriel Terra imprisoned many people he considered a threat to his rule. He sent some of them to Isla de Flores. On this small island off Uruguay's southern coast, Uruguayan professors, people critical of Terra's regime, and other so-called political enemies were isolated and unable to escape.

joined World War II (1939–1945) in February 1945 on the side of the Allies (the countries fighting against Germany). Baldomir may have hoped to generate goodwill among other Allies by joining the war. But at this point, the war was nearly over. Germany surrendered just a few months later. When Japan (another enemy of the Allies) also surrendered, the war ended.

At the end of 1951, Uruguayans voted for a new constitution. This document replaced the president with a nine-member executive body called the National Council of Government. The council included six members of the party that had won the most recent elections and three members of the runner-up party. Within the council, the role of president moved from one member of the dominant party to another each year. Under this system, the Colorado and Blanco parties shared power more equally. The nation's politics became more peaceful and stable than they had been in many decades. In 1958 the Blancos won a national election—their first national victory in ninety-three years.

But after a prosperous period, Uruguay's economy began to decline during the 1950s. Worldwide prices fell for beef and wool—still the country's most important exports. At the same time, the cost of imports increased. Inflation (rising prices combined with a drop in currency's value) increased dramatically. Many people lost their jobs. The National

Council of Government proved unable to solve these problems.

## Tupamaro Terrorism and Military Rule

As Uruguay's economic problems increased in the 1950s and 1960s, its peace shattered once again. A well-organized terrorist movement called the Tupamaros emerged. The Tupamaros were dissatisfied with Uruguay's government and society. Their goal was to bring greater social justice to Uruguay. For example, they wanted to strengthen labor unions (organizations that represent and support workers). They also believed that the government was weak and corrupt.

The Tupamaros challenged law and order in Uruguay. They robbed banks and other businesses. Then they gave some of the stolen money to poor Uruguayans. They also stole and publicized secret government records that proved political corruption. As they gained popularity among poor and disadvantaged Uruguayans, they began recruiting young men and women from the country's middle class.

Amid this unrest, in 1966 Uruguayans voted for a new constitution that replaced the rotating council with a more traditional presidential system. In that year, the Colorados returned to power. General Oscar Gestido, a retired military officer, became president. Before he died, after just nine months in office, Gestido significantly increased the size of Uruguay's police and armed forces.

Under the Colorado successors in office, all-out war against the Tupamaros developed. Although the Tupamaros had originally avoided using violence, they now changed their tactics. They used kidnapping and murder to draw attention to their cause.

Uruguay's police forces cracked down on the Tupamaros, with the help of a U.S. agency called the Office of Public Safety (OPS). Some observers charged that the tactics of the police and the OPS violated human rights. But the Uruguayan government continued its approach, desperate to bring down the Tupamaros. President Juan María Bordaberry Arocena began reducing the people's rights in an effort to gain control. He also strengthened the nation's military and used it to fight the rebels. The military was accused of using torture, as they arrested hundreds of people—many innocent—on suspicion of terrorism. The military soon grew to be the dominant force in the nation's government. In June 1973, military leaders closed down the legislature and seized control of the government.

The military dictatorship held Uruguay in its grip for more than a decade. It suppressed opposition using fear and violence. The leaders and their military and police forces arrested hundreds of political prisoners, often torturing or killing them. Many of these prisoners were innocent. Because some were kidnapped and their fates were often unknown, they came to be known as the "disappeared." The dictatorship also limited civil rights such as free speech.

By the early 1980s, under President Gregorio Alvarez, economic troubles plagued the country and its military-backed government. Huge protests against the regime erupted. Workers organized massive strikes, or work stoppages. Facing enormous unpopularity and pressure, military leaders finally agreed to release their grip on power. General democratic elections were planned for November 1984.

Colorado party leader Julio María Sanguinetti won the 1984 election. He took office in early 1985 as the country's new civilian (non-

After a parade, Uruguayan **President Gregorio Alvarez** (center, in suit) walks with his military government. Alvarez led a military regime from 1981 to 1985, when Julio María Sanguinetti took office.

military) president. The government released political prisoners and legalized all political parties. Sanguinetti still faced labor trouble, however. Fearful of unemployment and a rising cost of living, public and private laborers demanded higher wages. Workers also opposed the government's plan to privatize state-owned industries, or to sell them to individual, private buyers. Sanguinetti lost the 1989 election to Luis Alberto Lacalle of the Blanco party. Lacalle organized a coalition (mixed) government that included members of both political parties.

Despite labor unions' objections, Lacalle made plans to sell more industries to private investors. To control inflation, he also refused to give workers a raise in pay. Gradually, inflation lessened, and Uruguay's economy began to stabilize. But a public vote in December 1992 blocked Lacalle's effort to sell the national telephone company. The vote dealt a serious blow to the president's economic policies and his popularity.

## Ongoing Developments

In 1994 voters brought Julio María Sanguinetti back to office. These national elections also brought a new political party into the spotlight. The Encuentro Progresista (meaning "Progressive Encounter" and shortened to EP) took close to one-third of the presidential and legislative votes in that year.

Protests marked Sanguinetti's second presidential term. In May 1997, about twenty thousand people held a rally in Montevideo. They called for the government and military to release information about missing Uruguayan citizens. They believed that the military dictatorship of the 1970s had kidnapped, tortured, or killed these people. But the government did little in response. Two years later, about fifteen thousand people took part in another major protest. It was only when Jorge Batlle was elected in 1999 that the nation's leaders began addressing the matter. Batlle's administration formed a group to investigate what had happened to the Uruguayans who had disappeared during the military's rule.

Meanwhile, the nation's economy continued to suffer. Strikers and protesters demanded better health care, lower unemployment, and less privatization of national businesses. And in late 2001, Argentina went through its own economic crisis. The large nation's economy affected the whole region, and hardship in Uruguay increased. In addition to worker unrest, the nation faced a sudden flood of citizens moving to other countries for better opportunities.

The shaky economic situation dragged on into the elections of 2004. Tabaré Vázquez Rosas won, becoming the first president from

**President Tabaré Vázquez Rosas** *(left)* **and his vice president, Rodolfo Nin Novoa, wave to a crowd of supporters in 2005.**

the relatively young Frente Amplio (FA) party. Frente Amplio means "Broad Front" in Spanish. Vázquez pledged that he would work hard to stabilize the economy and also to eliminate poverty and unemployment in Uruguay. He also continued the investigation into the disappearances of Uruguayans in the 1970s. In 2006 the government made its first arrests in connection with the kidnappings and other human rights abuses of the former military dictatorship. Several former officers from Uruguay's military and police forces were arrested for the 1976 kidnapping of an Argentine citizen in Uruguay.

The nation's fortunes got a slight boost in 2008, when natural gas was discovered off Uruguay's coast. Experts believed that oil might exist there as well. It was not yet clear how large or of what quality the reserves of gas were. However, officials announced that in 2009 the nation would begin allowing private companies to investigate and tap the reserves. If significant reserves exist, they would provide Uruguay's first major source of energy other than hydroelectric power. Despite these discoveries, Uruguay's economy is far from stable and is still a focus of government effort.

## ◉ Government

The modern structure of Uruguay's government dates back to the 1966 constitution. This document established a system in which citizens eighteen years of age and older elect a president and vice president for five-year terms. The president serves as the head of state and acts with the advice of a fourteen-member council of ministers. The president appoints these ministers. The president may not run for a second consecutive term but can run again later.

The General Assembly is Uruguay's legislature, which writes and passes the nation's laws. It consists of two houses: a senate and a chamber of deputies. The people elect the thirty members of the senate (plus the vice president) to five-year terms. The chamber of deputies has ninety-nine members, also elected nationally.

When it's election time, most Uruguayans are eager to take part in their nation's democratic process. In most elections since the 1990s, more than 80 percent of Uruguayan men and women have turned out to vote.

Uruguay's Supreme Court—the nation's highest court of law—consists of a chief justice and four associate justices. The nation's General Assembly appoints these judges, who serve five-year terms. Like the president and vice president, Supreme Court justices may not immediately serve another term of office. They must wait at least five years between terms. Uruguay's top court decides whether laws passed by the federal and local governments follow the constitution. The Supreme Court also appoints judges for all lower courts and all justices of the peace.

Each of Uruguay's departments has its own council, as well as a legislative assembly. The department of Montevideo has a sixty-five-member assembly and a seven-member council. The nation's other departments have thirty-one-member assemblies and five-member councils. These departmental councils appoint local five-member councils to govern towns within each department.

Visit www.vgsbooks.com for links to websites with additional information about the current political situation in Uruguay.

# THE PEOPLE

The small nation of Uruguay is home to 3.3 million people. The nation's population is growing slowly, increasing only about 0.5 percent each year. If it continues to grow at this rate, Uruguay will have about 3.7 million residents in 2050.

Uruguay has a population density of 49 people per square mile (19 per sq. km)—a little less than South America's average of 57 people per square mile (22 per sq. km). By comparison, in Uruguay's neighbor Brazil, about 60 people live in every square mile (23 per sq. km). The United States has a density of 83 people per square mile (32 per sq. km).

Uruguay's population is not evenly distributed around the country. It is overwhelmingly concentrated in the nation's cities, especially in and around Montevideo. Altogether, about 94 percent of Uruguayans live in urban areas.

Like all nations, Uruguay has some poor citizens. During most of the twentieth century, it did not have wide extremes of wealth or poverty. Economic troubles in the 1990s and early 2000s did widen the gap

between rich and poor. Nevertheless, most modern Uruguayans have adequate food, housing, and medical care. The nation's cities have fewer slums (crowded, poor urban districts) than most Latin American countries. Only the poorest city dwellers lack electricity, running water, and sewers.

## ◉ Ethnic Groups

By far the largest ethnic group in Uruguay consists of people of European ancestry. About 88 percent of the nation's people were either born in Europe or have ancestors who were born there. Of these European descendants, most came from Spain. The nation's main cultural traditions are Spanish, reflecting the heritage of the earliest immigrants.

The next-largest group of European descendants in Uruguay is of Italian ancestry. Many other European nationalities also make up the country's population. They include Portuguese, French, German,

*Above:* Many **Uruguayans** have European ancestry. *Right:* A direct **descendant of the Charrúa** people participates in a traditional festival.

Dutch, Russian, Swedish, and many more. Since the early nineteenth century, many British immigrants have settled in Uruguay.

The country's original inhabitants, the Charrúa people, spent more than a century resisting Spanish and Portuguese colonization. But in the end, the colonists or their diseases killed nearly all of the Charrúa. Only about 8 percent of modern Uruguay's people claim indigenous heritage—and none are of 100 percent Charrúa ancestry. Nevertheless, these Charrúa descendants are proud of their heritage.

Blacks comprise about 4 percent of Uruguay's population. Most are the descendants of slaves brought from Africa to South America in the 1700s and 1800s. While there is little open discrimination against blacks, few are found in the upper ranks of government, business, or the professions. In modern Uruguay, they have demanded greater representation and respect.

## Languages

Reflecting Spain's dominant influence in Uruguay, the country's official language is Spanish. Most Uruguayans speak a dialect (language variation) of Spanish that reflects influences from Italian and other languages that immigrants brought to Uruguay. This dialect is sometimes called Rioplatense Spanish, referring to its origins in the Río de la Plata region.

Along Uruguay's Brazilian border, some people speak a mixture of Spanish and Portuguese (the national language of Brazil). Some of the names for this combined language are Riverense Portuñol, Brazilero, and Fronterizo.

In addition, some of Uruguay's non-Spanish European descendants still speak their native languages. Italian, Portuguese, and German are all heard in modern Uruguay. The language that the Charrúa people spoke is extinct.

## Health

Uruguay's health care system, for the most part, functions smoothly and well. The country has an estimated 365 doctors per 100,000 Uruguayans. Neighboring Argentina has about 301 per 100,000 people, while the United States has about 256. In addition, nearly all citizens have access to clean water and adequate sanitation facilities, such as indoor toilets and sewer systems.

Health statistics reflect this strong system. For example, less than 2.5 percent of the population is undernourished (lacks enough nourishing food). And the nation has an infant mortality rate of 10.5 deaths for every 1,000 live births—the second-lowest rate in South America, which has an average of 23. The average life expectancy for Uruguayans is 76 years of age. Women generally live slightly longer, with an average life expectancy of 79 years, while men have an average life expectancy of 72 years.

Of course, Uruguayans do get sick. Heart disease, cancer, tuberculosis (a lung disease), and measles affect some of the population. In addition, about 0.6 percent of Uruguayans have the human

Children in a rural school in Uruguay work on their laptops. Uruguay was one of the first countries to participate in the **One Laptop Per Child project,** started in 2007. The project enabled countries to buy inexpensive computers for their schools.

immunodeficiency virus (HIV) or acquired immunodeficiency syndrome (AIDS).

## Education

Uruguay boasts one of the best education systems in South America. One sign of this success is the nation's literacy rate (the number of adults who can read and write a basic sentence). Uruguay's adult literacy rate is about 97 percent, with slightly higher rates in cities than in rural areas.

The government runs free public schools from kindergarten through college. Although private schools exist, they follow guidelines set down by the state. Laws require schooling for all Uruguayan children between the ages of 6 and 14. In practice, not all school-age children actually attend classes. Older children, especially, may leave school to help their parents on ranches or with other work. But close to 90 percent of all school-age children in Uruguay do go to school.

Uruguay's students and teachers get their own days of recognition. September 21 is Student's Day, and Teacher's Day is September 22.

Primary school in Uruguay lasts for six years. At the age of 12, students move on to secondary school, which also lasts for six years. High school students can choose between two different kinds of schools. One type continues the academic programs offered in earlier grades and prepares students for college. The other kind of high school offers vocational and technical training, teaching students specific trades and job skills. These schools provide education in fields such as carpentry, electricity, radio repair, nursing, and automobile mechanics. In rural areas, vocational schools teach students about animal breeding, methods of raising crops, and dairy farming.

For those students who want to pursue higher education, Uruguay has several colleges and universities. The oldest and largest is the public University of the Republic, founded in 1849. More than 70,000 students attend the school, which has its main campus in Montevideo and smaller ones in other cities. The university offers degrees in law, medicine, engineering, architecture, sciences, social studies, and much more. Another major university is the private Catholic University. Like the University of the Republic, it has several campuses (including one in the capital) and offers a wide variety of degrees.

Visit www.vgsbooks.com for links to websites with additional information about schools and education in Uruguay.

## City Life and Country Life

The vast majority of Uruguay's population is urban, and Montevideo alone holds close to one-third of the country's people. Many residents of the capital and other large cities live in apartment buildings. Others have individual family homes, often with a small patio or yard where families enjoy the country's mild weather.

City dwellers have jobs in offices, shops, schools, factories, and a variety of other workplaces. Many residents of Montevideo work for the government. In their

People eat at a **sidewalk café** in Montevideo.

Some **gauchos** ride untamed horses in rodeo competitions. These are popular events in Uruguay.

free time, urban Uruguayans might see movies, attend concerts, dine out at restaurants, or visit with friends at cafés.

Although Uruguay's rural population is relatively small, it is very important to the nation's culture and economy. Most people in the Uruguayan countryside are hardworking farmers and ranchers. In contrast to many of the campesinos (farm workers) of other Latin American nations—who often struggle to make ends meet—Uruguayan farmers tend some of the most prosperous lands in South America. They are generally well educated and live comfortably. Most rural families reside in farmhouses or ranches set close to their fields or pastureland.

One of the most famous symbols of Uruguay's countryside is the gaucho. The legendary cowboy of South American stories wore a long woolen poncho (a woven shoulder cape with a hole in the center for the wearer's head) that streamed behind him as his horse galloped across the plains. He rode hard and often fought his rivals with a *facón* (a large knife). But this image is both exaggerated and outdated. Most modern gauchos wear blue jeans and jackets. And while horseback riding is still a popular sport in Uruguay, gauchos are more likely to drive a jeep or truck when working. Many gauchos carry radios so that they can listen to music or talk shows during long days in the pastures. In addition, they often carry thermoses of hot water for making maté, a tealike beverage high in caffeine. They have also added more vegetables to their once meat-heavy diet. But while Uruguay's gaucho has changed over the years, the memory of the old-time gaucho is still a large part of the nation's heritage.

A **farming family** stands inside a greenhouse.

## ▶ Women and Families

Many Uruguayan women work outside the home. The nation's laws officially protect them from discrimination. However, in practice, women do face prejudice when seeking jobs and promotions. Men hold most of the nation's most prominent and high-paying jobs. In addition, domestic violence is a problem, with some women suffering abuse by their husbands.

Most Uruguayans have relatively small families, usually with one to three children. Grandparents have a close relationship with this family unit, sometimes living in the same home. Grandparents also often help with child rearing. In addition, family reunions that bring together a wider circle of relatives are common. Many families gather annually for these events.

Uruguayan women won the right to vote in 1932. One decade later, in 1942, voters elected the first Uruguayan women to hold political office. That year, two women won seats in the nation's senate, and two others joined the chamber of deputies.

# CULTURAL LIFE

Spanish influence strongly flavors Uruguay's cultural life. Other European and African traditions have also made their mark. And the Charrúa people, though virtually extinct in modern Uruguay, left behind their own cultural legacy. These elements appear in Uruguay's music, dance, literature, religion, social customs, and more.

## ▷ Religion

European colonists brought Christianity, specifically Roman Catholicism, to Uruguay centuries ago. As a result, most Uruguayans define themselves as Christian. Although the statistics vary, about 54 percent of Uruguayans state that they are Catholic. An estimated 11 percent follow Protestantism, a non-Catholic branch of Christianity that includes many different denominations. But in practice, most Christian Uruguayans are not regular churchgoers.

Uruguay is also home to a small Jewish community, which makes up about 1 percent of the population. Most Uruguayan Jews live in

Montevideo, and the capital has several synagogues (Jewish places of worship) as well as a Jewish cemetery.

About another 1 percent or less of Uruguayans follow religions with African origins, such as Umbanda. This faith combines African religious traditions with aspects of Christianity. It began among Brazil's black residents but spread to other South American nations.

A small number of people in the remaining 33 percent of Uruguayans follow other religions, such as Mormonism (Church of Jesus Christ of Latter-day Saints), Buddhism, Islam, or the Bahai faith. Others believe in God but do not belong to a specific religion. An additional segment of the population does not believe in God.

Since the constitution of 1919, church and state have been strictly separate in Uruguay. Public schools must not teach or promote religion, and the country has no official national religion. Politically, the Roman Catholic Church uses the Christian Democratic Party—a relatively small group—to voice its ideas and goals.

Uruguayans honor Iemanjá, the goddess of the sea, in an **Umbanda** celebration. The Umbanda religion combines elements of Christianity and African traditions.

## ◉ Holidays and Festivals

Due to Uruguay's history with Catholicism, most people celebrate Christian holidays. But their celebrations are often less focused on church and religion than in most Latin American countries. Christmas, celebrating the birth of Jesus, falls during Uruguay's summer. The day includes time with relatives, gift giving, a special family meal, and late-night fireworks. Other important dates on the Christian calendar include Easter and Holy Week (the week ending on Easter Sunday). Many people in Latin America spend this time going to church and observing the holiday with religious traditions. But Uruguay's more secular (nonreligious) people celebrate in other ways. During these days, many businesses close. A great number of Uruguayans go to the beaches or countryside for a relaxing getaway.

One of the country's most vibrant and popular celebrations

### MERRY FAMILY DAY!

Because many Uruguayans do not practice religion, even the biggest Christian holidays often go by nonreligious names. For example, Uruguayans sometimes call Christmas Family Day. Similarly, Holy Week is also known as Semana de Turismo (Tourism Week), and many families do take the week off to travel.

A **costumed dancer** plays the drums in a Carnival parade.

is Carnival, a two-day festival before the beginning of Lent (a forty-day period leading up to Easter). During Carnival, parades with flowered floats and marchers in brightly colored masks and costumes fill the streets. Streamers and colored lights adorn buildings. People set up decorated stages called *tablados* in each neighborhood. These stages then host performances by musicians, clowns, dancers, and masked actors. At the end of Carnival, the best tablado presentations win awards.

Uruguayans also observe a variety of secular holidays. For example, in April the country celebrates the Landing of the Thirty-Three Immortals. This event commemorates the deeds of the rebels who fought for Uruguay's independence. Winter, especially, brings many special occasions. June 19 is the birthday of General José Artigas, July 18 is Constitution Day, and August 25 is Independence Day. Many people do not have to work on these days, and sometimes parades or speeches mark the holidays.

## Literature

In Uruguay's pre-Columbian years (before Christopher Columbus's exploration of the New World), the Charrúa people had their own, nonwritten stories. They told legends, such as a story about the creation of the world and people. Many of these tales explained events in the natural world around them.

In colonial Uruguay, most writers wrote in styles and about themes that were similar to those of European authors. However, in the late nineteenth century, local writers began to develop a unique Uruguayan style. This new style reflected their country's traditions, history, and culture. One of the first authors in this trend was José Alonso y Trelles. He wrote about gauchos and tried to reproduce their dialect. Another influential Uruguayan writer is José Enrique Rodó, who was born in 1872. Rodó wrote a philosophical essay called *Ariel* that became widely known and admired. The essay deals with the interaction between human reason and spirit. Florencio Sánchez, born in 1875, was a famous playwright who also worked as a journalist.

Montevideo's Teatro Solís was founded in 1856—making it the oldest operating theater in North or South America. Named for Juan Díaz de Solís, the theater still presents operas, concerts, and ballets.

Juan Zorrilla de San Martín is among Uruguay's most famous male poets. He wrote his works about the same time as Rodó. Zorrilla de San Martín's epic poem *Tabaré* was published in 1888. It tells the story of a Spanish girl and an indigenous Uruguayan boy who fall in love. The tragic love story highlights the Charrúa people's fight for survival in the face of European colonization.

Women poets have also achieved recognition in Uruguay. For example, Juana de Ibarbourou (born in 1892) won many awards for her poetry. Many of her poems expressed feminist ideals, such as equality for men and women. She also looked to nature as an inspiration. Some of her work describes the parallel between the year's natural seasons and the human seasons of youth, maturity, old age, and death. Another female poet was Delmira Agustini. Her promising career came to an abrupt end when she was murdered in 1914, at the age of twenty-seven.

More recent writers include Mario Benedetti, who has written dozens of works, from poems to plays to novels. Eduardo Galeano is another prominent author. His works, which include novels and short stories, often explore Uruguayan history. And Carmen Posadas is an award-winning children's writer who has also written for adults, film, and television. Her works have been translated into many languages.

# Music and Dance

Uruguay's folk music is lively and often centers around familiar themes in gaucho legends. The country's earliest folk music arose from the lonely life of these gauchos, who sang their own songs of love and adventure. The rugged cowboys sang these tunes around the evening campfire to the accompaniment of guitars. Eventually, the music gave rise to the *pericón*, Uruguay's national dance. The pericón features several couples—usually eight—holding hands and dancing in one or two rows, using various sets of steps.

In the nineteenth century, a rich classical music tradition arose in Uruguay. Much of this music was heavily influenced by opera from Italy. The country's most famous composer was Eduardo Fabini (born in 1882). Although he studied music in Belgium, he drew his greatest inspiration from the beauty of Uruguay's countryside. Later composers include Hector Tosar Errecart. Born in 1923, Tosar Errecart was a child prodigy who had composed several works by the age of nineteen.

A group of musicians plays traditional Uruguayan tango music. The double bass *(left)* and *bandoneón (center)* are instruments typical of Uruguayan tango music.

In the 1950s, he won international acclaim for his piece *Danza Criolla* (*Creole Dance*). ("Creole" is an old name for Uruguayans of Spanish descent.) This classical work used themes from gaucho folklore.

The 1960s brought a period known as the Uruguayan Invasion. During these years, Uruguayan pop and rock groups hit the big time, becoming very popular not only in their home country but also in Argentina. These groups included Los Shakers and Los Mockers. Most modeled their music and their images after the British band the Beatles. The Beatles' huge success in the United States began a wave of popularity for British bands, which was called the British Invasion. Some of the Uruguayan Invasion bands sang in English.

One of Uruguay's most important local styles is candombe. It arose in the nation's black community in the early 1800s. It is based on African drumming and features several types of drums of different sizes and sounds. A group called a *cuerda*—sometimes made up of as many as one hundred drummers—performs candombe with these drums. Dancing accompanies the music, and usually acts out legends or stories featuring colorful characters. Candombe remains a popular and important part of Uruguayan culture.

Uruguayans continue to enjoy music in a variety of styles, from tango to jazz to hip-hop and rap. The country holds several annual music festivals that draw large crowds. Some of the most popular modern groups are the rock bands No Te Va Gustar and La Vela Puerca. These groups also attract many listeners in Argentina.

## SECRET SONGS

Candombe quickly became so popular and widespread among Uruguay's slaves that white Uruguayans worried that it would threaten their control. In 1808 some wealthy Uruguayans—claiming that candombe was immoral and also that it distracted slaves from their labor—wanted the music and dance banned. Black residents of Uruguay simply continued to enjoy candombe in secret, and it remained a strong cultural force through the centuries and into modern times.

Uruguayan painter Carlos Páez Vilaró leads a **cuerda of drummers** during a Carnival celebration. Each year, Páez Vilaró plays the drums with a Carnival band.

## ◉ Visual Arts

The earliest works of art in Uruguay are rock paintings and carvings that date back thousands of years. Some of these Charrúa artworks show abstract patterns. Others depict Uruguay's native wildlife.

During the colonial era, Uruguay's first prominent painter was Juan Manuel Blanes. He was born in Montevideo in 1830 and gained fame for his paintings illustrating the nation's history. In the early twentieth century, José Cuneo was an outstanding painter whose favorite subjects were moonlit landscapes. He used watercolors to depict these scenes. The works of twentieth-century painter Pedro Figari include scenes of black culture and community in Uruguay. For example, several of Figari's works show candombe musicians and dancers.

Famous Uruguayan sculptors have included José Luis Zorrilla de San Martín—son of the poet Juan Zorrilla de San Martín. Zorrilla de San Martín was born in Spain in 1891, but his Uruguayan family returned to their homeland when he was still a boy. Another prominent sculptor was José Belloni, born in 1882. Both of these artists created works reflecting themes of Uruguay's gaucho past.

More recently, one of Uruguay's best-known artists is Carlos Páez Vilaró. His lively and colorful works often reflect Uruguay's culture, people, and daily life. He gained attention in the United States for his 530-foot-long (162 m) mural in the Pan American Union building in Washington, D.C. Páez Vilaró is an artist of many talents.

In addition to painting, he sculpts, writes poetry, and composes music. Santiago Paulós is a young painter who has won awards and international recognition for his haunting portraits. Virginia Patrone also creates portraits, usually choosing women for her subjects.

## ◉ Sports and Recreation

By far the most popular sport in Uruguay is *futbol* (soccer). The country is home to many teams, the most popular of which are the rivals Peñarol and Nacional. These and other teams have many fiercely devoted fans. The national Uruguayan team is nicknamed the Charrúas. They have won many international competitions, such as the Copa América, a South American tournament. They have also played in the World Cup ten times. This large tournament brings together teams from all over the world every four years. Uruguay has won two World Cups. In fact, it won the very first one, which took place in Uruguay in 1930. The Uruguayan national team has also won two Olympic gold medals.

The Uruguayan national **futbol team** poses in 2007.

Uruguayans enjoy many other athletic pursuits. Horse riding is an old tradition in Uruguay, and horse racing and rodeos remain very popular. The country's rural areas are attractive places for hiking, and many Uruguayans enjoy boating and swimming in their nation's rivers and coastal waters. Tennis, golf, and basketball are also popular sports. Uruguay has sent athletes to the Olympic Games to compete in sports such as rowing, boxing, and cycling.

In addition to sports, Uruguay offers many other pleasant ways to spend free time. Especially in Montevideo, residents can enjoy a variety of live entertainment, such as theater, opera, and ballet.

Another popular option is going to the movies. Movies in Uruguay date back to about 1900, when Montevideo businessman Félix Oliver became the country's first filmmaker. Oliver made a short movie about a bicycle race. Modern Uruguay is home to actors and filmmakers, and Montevideo hosts an annual film festival that presents movies from all over the world.

Visit www.vgsbooks.com for links to websites with additional information about popular Uruguayan sports and other recreational activities. Follow the Uruguayan national futbol team, and see what events are happening in Montevideo.

## Food

Many typical Uruguayan dishes reflect the country's gaucho past and meat-eating tastes. Beef is central to the national diet. Especially popular is *asado*, barbecued beef or lamb rubbed with coarse salt and roasted on a spit over hot coals. Another meat dish is *parrillada*—a mixture of grilled sausage, kidney, and liver. To make a hearty stew called *puchero*, cooks boil a combination of meats, including bacon, with chickpeas (garbanzo beans) and various vegetables.

European influences also remain strong in Uruguay's food. Many Montevideo restaurants favor Italian and French cuisine. Pasta is especially popular with many diners of all ethnicities.

A diner on the go in Uruguay might grab a *chivito*, a steak sandwich that includes cheese, tomato, and other ingredients. The similar *choripán* features sausage called chorizo instead of steak. Another form of fast food is the empanada, a savory pastry filled with meat or fish.

A cook prepares a variety of meats on a **parrilla,** or grill, at a market in Uruguay. Barbecued meat is popular in Uruguayan dishes.

The national drink is yerba maté—a tea brewed from a species of native holly. Farmers and ranchers customarily drink maté from a gourd, with a silver straw called a *bombilla*. Many Uruguayans also drink coffee.

Dulce de leche—a caramelly concoction of cooked sugar and milk—is considered the national sweet. It is an ingredient in many of Uruguay's desserts and pastries, such as the *alfajor*. This sandwichlike dessert consists of two buttery cookies with a filling of dulce de leche. Custardlike flan topped with dulce de leche is another popular dessert. Some diners prefer *arroz con leche*, a sweet rice pudding with milk. And fresh fruit is always a fine way to end a Uruguayan meal.

Uruguayans drink **yerba maté** tea through bombilla straws. The straws have filters on the ends to strain the tea leaves.

# ALFAJORES

These cookies are a Uruguayan favorite.

**Dulce de leche:**

**14-ounce can of sweetened condensed milk**

**½ cup cornstarch**

**¼ teaspoon baking powder**

**⅛ teaspoon salt**

**Cookies:**

**1 egg**

**1 stick (½ cup) butter**

**½ teaspoon vanilla extract**

**¼ cup sugar**

**powdered sugar for dusting**

**1 to 1¼ cups all-purpose flour**

1. To make the dulce de leche, preheat the oven to 425°F (220°C).
2. Pour the sweetened condensed milk into a glass pie plate or shallow baking dish. Set the pie plate in a larger, deeper pan, such as a roasting pan. Add hot water to the large pan until it reaches halfway up the side of the pie plate.
3. Cover the pie plate snugly with aluminum foil and bake for 1 to 1¼ hours. Check a few times during baking and add more water to the roasting pan as necessary.
4. Once the dulce de leche is thick and browned, carefully remove from the oven and let cool. Once cool, whisk until smooth.
5. To make the cookies, lower the oven heat to 350°F (180°C).
6. Beat the butter and sugar until light and fluffy. In another bowl, whisk together the flour (starting with 1 cup), cornstarch, baking powder, and salt. Set aside these dry ingredients.
7. Add the egg and vanilla to the butter and beat until smooth. Add the dry ingredients and beat until the dough comes together. Add some of the remaining ¼ cup of flour if the dough is very sticky.
8. On a clean, floured surface, roll out the dough to about ⅛-inch thickness. If the dough begins to stick to the surface or the rolling pin, dust with more flour. Use a round cookie cutter or the mouth of a small glass to cut out cookies. Place on a baking sheet and bake for 12 to 15 minutes or until the edges are light golden brown. Place on a rack to cool.
9. When the cookies are cool, spread some dulce de leche (about 1 to 1½ teaspoons) on the bottom of one cookie. Place another cookie on top of the dulce de leche to make a sandwich. Repeat until all cookies have been used. Dust with powdered sugar.

Makes about 20 alfajores

# THE ECONOMY

Uruguay has generally enjoyed a stable and healthy economy. Especially in contrast to other South American nations, which have often struggled with money matters, Uruguay has had a smooth path. However, in the late 1990s, the nation entered a recession (economic slowdown) that dragged into the early 2000s. The country's people faced rapid inflation as the cost of goods went up and the value of the nation's currency (the Uruguayan peso) went down.

The nation also struggled with debt, caused in part by a trade deficit (when a nation's imports are of greater value than its exports). Uruguay had also borrowed money from other countries, especially to cover the cost of importing oil for energy. Uruguayan politicians and economists worked to improve the situation. They used measures such as selling government-owned businesses, or privatization, and raising taxes. The nation also received special loans from international financial agencies such as the International Monetary Fund (IMF). The IMF carefully monitors loans to help nations strengthen their economies and

pay back debt. By about 2006, the tactics seemed to have worked, and Uruguay's economy was stronger and was growing once again.

## Services and Trade

Uruguay's service industry is the largest area of its economy. It accounts for about 58 percent of the country's gross domestic product. (Abbreviated as GDP, gross domestic product is a measure of the total annual value of goods and services produced by a nation's workers.) Activities in the service sector include government work, banking, insurance, health care, retail sales, tourism, and other jobs that supply services rather than producing goods. This large sector also employs 74 percent of all the nation's workers.

Tourism is a major part of the nation's service sector and a valuable source of foreign income. Most visitors come from Argentina, Brazil, and other nations in South and Central America. A smaller number arrive from the United States, Europe, and elsewhere.

Popular vacation spots, such as this beach in Punta del Este, draw crowds of tourists and generate revenue for the country.

These visitors enjoy Uruguay's beaches, its countryside, and the many sights of Montevideo.

Foreign trade is another important aspect of Uruguay's economy. Many of Uruguay's exports are agricultural, such as animal hides, wool, beef, and crops such as corn and sugarcane. The nation also exports manufactured items such as textiles and processed foods. In 1991 Uruguay joined with Argentina, Brazil, and Paraguay to form the Mercado Común del Sur (Mercosur), a common trading market in southern South America. By joining Mercosur, these nations ended all trade barriers, including tariffs (taxes on trade items), among themselves in 1995. As a result, Uruguay trades largely with other Mercosur nations, and its single most important customer for

## HOME ON THE RANGE

A popular activity for many tourists in Uruguay is a stay on a ranch, or estancia. While there, visitors can ride horses, enjoy the beauty of Uruguay's countryside, and lounge in luxurious rooms. One of the nation's most prominent and historic estancias is San Pedro de Timote. Located in south-central Uruguay, it dates back to 1854.

exports is Brazil. The United States also imports many Uruguayan goods, as do Argentina, Mexico, Germany, and Italy.

Uruguay also imports goods such as machinery, fuel, chemicals, and metals. The country buys most of its imports from Argentina and Brazil.

## Agriculture, Fishing, and Forestry

Livestock raising and farming are an important and long-standing part of Uruguay's economic activities. This sector, plus fishing and forestry, accounts for only about 10 percent of the nation's GDP. It employs just 5 percent of Uruguayan workers. But sales from meat, wool, and hides have long accounted for most of the nation's exports. The fortunes of the Uruguayan economy rise and fall with the fluctuations of world prices for meat and wool.

Together, cattle and sheep in Uruguay outnumber people by more than 6 to 1.

About 75 percent of all the nation's land is devoted to raising animals. About 12 million cattle roam these pasturelands, along with close to 10 million sheep. Some farmers also raise pigs, chickens, and horses.

Another 8 to 10 percent of Uruguay's land supports crops. The nation's main crops include rice, wheat, corn, barley, and sugarcane. Uruguayan farmers also grow fruits such as oranges, tangerines, lemons, apples, and grapes. Vegetables including tomatoes, carrots, and potatoes also thrive.

In addition to being vulnerable to changing prices for their goods, Uruguay's farmers face a variety of other dangers. Animal disease is one threat. In 2001 the nation's livestock suffered an outbreak of foot-and-mouth disease, which is highly contagious among cattle, sheep, and other livestock. The disease brought Uruguay's profitable meat exports to a halt until 2003. Weather variations can also be problems. In late 2008 and early 2009, Uruguay experienced a severe drought. The dry spell caused crop losses, resulting in rising food prices. When droughts last for a very long time, they can also cause livestock deaths and a shortage of hydroelectricity as river levels drop.

Uruguay's rivers, lakes, and coastal waters support a small but profitable fishing industry. Fish along the coast include Argentine hake, whitemouth croaker, striped weakfish, and Patagonian toothfish. Squid and crab also come from the coastal waters, while the nation's rivers are home to the dorado, a large salmonlike fish. Total annual catches average more than 130,000 tons (117,934 metric tons). Uruguay exports about half of this amount.

A **fisherman** stands in a fishing boat docked in the Punta del Este harbor.

Uruguay also has a small forestry sector. Pine and eucalyptus are the most commonly cut trees. Most logged trees become pulp to make paper or other products. Others become fuel or are used in construction or furniture making.

## ▷ Manufacturing and Mining

Uruguay's manufacturing sector is relatively small. Together, manufacturing and mining make up about 32 percent of GDP. They employ about 21 percent of the country's labor force. Factories—mostly in Montevideo and the surrounding area—produce goods such as textiles, food and beverage products, and chemicals. Fray Bentos, in western Uruguay, was the site of the nation's first large meatpacking plant, which opened in the early 1860s. The city is still home to food-processing plants and other industries.

Uruguay's mining sector is also small. The nation does have some

### CORNED BEEF FOR EVERYONE!

Uruguay's Fray Bentos meatpacking plant became famous in the 1900s for exporting its products. The most widespread of these exports was corned beef. Fray Bentos corned beef was especially important during World Wars I and II, when it fed many soldiers in Europe. In fact, Fray Bentos's impact was so great that it earned the nickname Kitchen of the World.

Textile workers at the Casa Mario leather factory, the largest and oldest leather factory in the world

deposits of minerals and metals such as gypsum (a mineral used in fertilizers and construction), silver, and gold. But these deposits are minimal, and so far the country has no large-scale mining industry.

## Transportation

Uruguay has a well developed system of highways and roads. More than 4,500 miles (7,242 km) of paved roads crisscross the small nation, along with many more unpaved routes. The most important highway leads west out of Montevideo to Colonia del Sacramento, on the Río de la Plata, before swinging west and north to pass Mercedes, a major market city, and Fray Bentos, hub of the meatpacking industry. The road then goes on to Paysandú (a port on the Uruguay River for ocean-going ships), Salto (a port for coastal shipping), and eventually Artigas on the Brazilian border.

East from Montevideo, another major highway leads to Chuy, a small town on the Brazilian border. This highway is a major commercial route within Uruguay. It is also part of the most heavily traveled land route on the eastern coast of South America. The highway connects six major cities—Río de Janeiro, São Paulo, Curitiba, Pôrto Alegre (all in Brazil), Montevideo, and Buenos Aires. Buses keep tight schedules along this 1,000-mile-long (1,609 km) run from Río de Janeiro to Buenos Aires, as do big trucks carrying products to and from the major urban markets. From Montevideo, other roads lead into the

The **Puente de las Americas,** a bridge built in 2005, leads into Montevideo.

interior of the country. These routes carry farm produce and livestock to the capital. The nation also has more than 1,250 miles (2,012 km) of railroads.

Uruguay's largest airport is Carrasco International Airport, in Montevideo. It provides both domestic and international flights, including daily flights to Brazil and Argentina. Smaller airports also dot the country.

Water transportation remains important in Uruguay, though mainly for shipping goods rather than for helping people travel from place to place. The nation has several ocean ports at Montevideo and other coastal cities, as well as ports on the Uruguay River.

## ◉ Media and Communications

Uruguay has a strong system of communications and media. Uruguayans can tune in to dozens of radio stations to hear music, news, talk shows, and more. They also have their choice of a wide variety of television stations. In addition to local Uruguayan radio and television, the nation receives signals from stations transmitting from nearby cities in Argentina and Brazil.

Montevideo has several daily newspapers, many of which are directly tied to political parties or factions. For example, *El País*, one of the nation's most popular papers, is the official publication of the Blanco party. Altogether Uruguay produces more than fifty newspapers, with an estimated total circulation of close to 1 million readers.

More and more Uruguayans get their news and information from the Internet. Many people have access to the Internet at home. In addition, Montevideo and some of the nation's other cities offer Internet cafés where people can get on-line and have a coffee at the same time.

Modern technology has also affected the way people get in touch with one another. Many people are using cellular phones in addition to or instead of older telephone lines. While more than 900,000 telephone lines are in use around the country, it is estimated that more than 2 million or possibly even 3 million people have cell phone service.

**In 2009 Uruguay is estimated to have more than 1 million Internet users—and the number is steadily rising. In 2005 the figure was estimated at about 680,000 users.**

Visit www.vgsbooks.com for links to websites with additional information about media in Uruguay. Link to local online newspapers, and learn about what is happening throughout the country.

## The Future

Over the centuries, Uruguay has confronted many issues. Colonialism, independence, the transition from dictatorship to democracy, and internal strife have each presented their own challenges. Economic issues came to the fore in the 1990s. Rising unemployment and inflation plagued the population and Uruguayan businesses. And ongoing emigration threatened to rob the country of some of its smart and educated people.

But Uruguayans have overcome each obstacle in their way. Modern Uruguay remains one of South America's most prosperous and stable nations. Looking ahead, the Uruguayan people draw strength and inspiration from their past—from both the fierce Charrúa warrior and the independent gaucho. Uruguayans remain hopeful that their homeland offers them a bright and promising future.

## Timeline

| | |
|---|---|
| 15,000–10,000 B.C. | Humans begin settling in South America. |
| A.D. 1492 | Christopher Columbus reaches the New World. |
| 1516 | Juan Díaz de Solís sails up the Río de la Plata and arrives in Uruguay. Indigenous people kill him and most of his party. |
| 1520 | Ferdinand Magellan sails along Uruguay's coast. |
| 1527 | Sebastian Cabot names the Río de la Plata. |
| EARLY 1600S | Hernando Arias de Saavedra introduces cattle and horses to Uruguay's plains. |
| 1624 | Catholic missionaries arrive in Uruguay. |
| 1680 | The Portuguese found a settlement at Colonia del Sacramento. |
| 1726 | Spanish settlers found Montevideo. |
| MID-1700S | Colonists in the Americas import slaves from Africa. |
| 1776 | Spain creates the Viceroyalty of the Río de la Plata. |
| 1808 | British forces take control of Montevideo. This same year, Uruguayan elites attempt to ban candombe music. |
| 1815 | José Artigas and his gaucho rebels declare independence, though they do not succeed in winning it. |
| 1825 | The Thirty-Three Immortals invade Uruguay with the aim of winning their homeland's independence. |
| 1828 | Uruguay becomes independent. |
| 1830 | Uruguay's first constitution comes into effect on July 18. |
| 1831 | Uruguayan soldiers ambush and kill most remaining Charrúa at Salsipuedes Creek. |
| 1839 | The Guerra Grande begins. During the course of the long war, slavery is abolished in Uruguay. |
| 1849 | The University of the Republic is founded in Montevideo. |
| 1856 | Montevideo's Teatro Solis is founded. |
| 1865–1870 | Uruguay fights alongside Brazil and Argentina, against Paraguay, in the War of the Triple Alliance. |
| 1888 | Juan Zorrilla de San Martín's poem *Tabaré* is published. |

| 1900 | Félix Oliver makes a short film about a bicycle race, becoming Uruguay's first filmmaker. |
|---|---|
| 1903 | José Batlle y Ordóñez becomes president. He implements wide-ranging reforms. |
| 1914-1918 | World War I takes place. |
| 1930s | A worldwide economic slowdown hurts Uruguay's exports and economy. |
| 1930 | Uruguay hosts and wins the first World Cup soccer tournament, beating Argentina in the final match. |
| 1932 | Uruguayan women win the right to vote. |
| 1939-1945 | World War II takes place. |
| 1949 | Builders complete Uruguay's first hydroelectric plant, located on the Río Negro. |
| 1950 | Uruguay wins its second World Cup, in a major upset against Brazil. |
| 1960s | The Tupamaros carry out bank robberies, kidnappings, and other disruptive and terrorist activities. |
| 1973 | A military dictatorship takes power. This regime kidnaps, tortures, and kills hundreds of Uruguayans. |
| 1984 | Democracy is restored in Uruguay. |
| 1991 | Uruguay and other South American nations form the trade organization Mercosur. |
| 1997 | A large rally in Montevideo calls for government investigation of the fate of Uruguayan citizens who disappeared during the military dictatorship of the 1970s. |
| 2004 | Tabaré Vázquez becomes the first president from the Frente Amplio (FA) party. |
| 2006 | The government makes its first arrests in connection with the crimes of the 1970s military dictatorship. |
| 2008 | Two ships collide off Uruguay's coast, causing an oil spill. In late 2008 Uruguay experiences a serious drought that lasts into 2009. |
| 2009 | Uruguay's soccer players go on strike, claiming that some players had not received their pay. |

**COUNTRY NAME** Eastern Republic of Uruguay

**AREA** 68,037 square miles (176,215 sq. km)

**MAIN LANDFORMS** Western Lowlands, Central Plateau, Coastal Plain, Cuchilla Grande, Cuchilla de Haedo

**HIGHEST POINT** Cerro Catedral, 1,686 feet (514 meters) above sea level

**MAJOR RIVERS** Cebollatí, Cuareim, Río Negro, Río de la Plata, Tacuarembó, Uruguay, Yaguarón, Yi

**ANIMALS** caimans, capybaras, dorados, giant anteaters, horneros, mulitas, nutrias, piranhas, rheas, seals, sea turtles, tortoises

**CAPITAL CITY** Montevideo

**OTHER MAJOR CITIES** Fray Bentos, Maldonado, Paysandú, Punta del Este, Salto

**OFFICIAL LANGUAGE** Spanish

**MONETARY UNIT** Uruguayan peso. 100 *centésimos* = 1 Uruguayan peso.

## URUGUAYAN CURRENCY

Uruguay officially adopted the modern Uruguayan peso (*peso uruguayo*) in 1993. But the nation's currency had been some form of the peso for more than two centuries. Coins come in denominations of 50 centésimos and 1, 2, 5, and 10 Uruguayan pesos. Banknotes come in denominations of 20, 50, 100, 200, 500, 1,000, and 2,000 Uruguayan pesos. Coins depict native wildlife, such as the mulita who strides across the 1-peso coin or the capybara on the 2-peso piece. Bills show historical figures. For example, the 20-peso bill bears the image of Juan Zorrilla de San Martín.

Uruguay's national flag was adopted on July 11, 1830—seven days before the country's first constitution came into effect. It consists of nine horizontal stripes of equal width, in alternating blue and white. These stripes symbolize Uruguay's original nine departments. The flag's colors echo those of Argentina's national flag, reflecting Uruguay's close historical ties to its southwestern neighbor. In the upper corner closest to the flagpole is the image of a yellow sun with a human face. Joaquín Suárez, who served as one of Uruguay's early presidents, designed the flag.

Uruguay's national anthem is titled "Orientales, la Patria o la tumba!" ("Uruguayans, the Fatherland or the Grave!"). It was adopted in 1845. Francisco Esteban Acuña de Figueroa wrote the words, and Francisco José Debali composed the music. This pair also wrote Paraguay's national anthem. The anthem is very long, consisting of eleven verses. Part of the anthem follows below in Spanish and English.

> Libertad, libertad, orientales
> este grito a la patria salvó
> y a sus bravos en fieras batallas
> de entusiasmo sublimé inflamó.
> De este don sacrosanto la gloria
> merecimos, tiranos: temblad!
> Libertad en la lid clamaremos
> y muriendo también libertad!

> Freedom, freedom, Uruguayans
> This cry saved our country
> And inflamed its brave men
> With sublime enthusiasm in fierce battles.
> We deserved the glory of this sacred gift.
> Tyrants: tremble!
> In the fight we shall clamor for freedom
> And, dying still cry for it!

> Visit www.vgsbooks.com for a link to a site where you can listen to Uruguay's national anthem, "Orientales, la Patria o la tumba!".

*Note: Some Uruguayans' last names follow the Spanish style. The father's last name comes first, followed by the mother's last name. The father's last name is used in the shortened form and for alphabetization. For example, Tabaré Vázquez Rosas takes the name Vázquez from his father and Rosas from his mother. In shortened form, he may be called Vázquez Rosas or simply Vázquez.*

**DELMIRA AGUSTINI** (1886–1914) Born in Montevideo to a family of Italian immigrants, Agustini soon proved to have a talent for writing. She started writing her own poems at the age of ten and soon began publishing them in Uruguayan journals such as *La Alborada* (*The Dawn*). Agustini's work drew attention from writers and critics in Uruguay and around South America. She published her first poetry book in 1907, *El Libro Blanco* (*The White Book*), at the age of twenty-one. She released another book just three years later, and a third book in 1913. Her life and career were cut short in 1914, when her husband (whom she had asked for a divorce) killed her. Nevertheless, Agustini remains one of Latin America's most important poets.

**JOSÉ GERVASIO ARTIGAS ARNAL** (1764–1850) Probably born in Montevideo (historians are not sure), Artigas was part of a wealthy family in colonial Uruguay. At an early age, he worked as a gaucho. He later joined in the fight against Spanish colonists in Uruguay, leading soldiers against Spain in 1811. He and his rebels declared independence in 1815 and briefly held power. Artigas was not ultimately successful in winning Uruguay's freedom, and he died in exile in Paraguay. Nevertheless, his efforts were important steps on the country's road to independence. He is one of Uruguay's most beloved heroes.

**DIEGO FORLÁN CORAZO** (b. 1979) Born in Montevideo, Forlán is one of Uruguay's most famous soccer players. Forlán showed talent as an athlete from his early years, proving himself to be a skilled tennis player. But he chose to follow in the footsteps of his father, Pablo Forlán, who played soccer for Uruguay in the 1966 and 1974 World Cups. The younger Forlán plays in the position of striker, also known as a forward. He has played for several teams in Uruguay and beyond, including England's famous Manchester United team and Spain's Atlético Madrid. Forlán participated in the 2002 World Cup on the Uruguayan national team and also played for Uruguay in the Copa América in 2004 and 2007.

**NATALIA OREIRO** (b. 1977) Born in Montevideo, Oreiro is a singer and actress. She began studying acting at an early age, and by the time she was a teenager, she had appeared in many television commercials. She has acted in several television shows as well as in an Argentine movie. By the age of twenty-two, Oreiro had released her first musical album, and she has released two more albums since then. Her music earned her a nomination for a Latin Grammy (one of Latin America's most famous music awards) and has won her many fans. She also continues to act in a variety of television programs. Oreiro is married to a fellow musician, Ricardo Mollo, who is in an Argentine rock band.

**VIRGINIA PATRONE** (b. 1950) Born in Montevideo, Patrone is one of Uruguay's noted modern artists. As a young woman, she was interested in architecture and studied the field at the University of the Republic. But she soon developed an interest in other forms of art and spent several years studying and exploring painting and etching. She creates fanciful portraits, mostly of women, and her art has appeared in shows and museums around the world. She has also taught art in schools from New York City to Madrid, Spain.

**PABLO STOLL** (b. 1974) Stoll was born in Montevideo. He attended the city's Catholic University, where he met fellow student Juan Pablo Rebella. Both young men were interested in filmmaking and soon began working together on short movies. After graduation they undertook longer projects. Together they wrote and directed the film *25 Watts*, released in 2001. This movie tells the story of one day in the lives of three young Montevideo residents. It went on to win awards at several international film festivals. Stoll and Rebella's next project was the film *Whisky*, released in 2004. It focused on a pair of brothers and their personal issues. Following Rebella's death in 2006, Stoll has continued to work in the film and television industries.

**TABARÉ VÁZQUEZ ROSAS** (b. 1940) Born in Montevideo, Vázquez was a good student and went to college at his hometown's University of the Republic. He studied medicine and went on to become an oncologist (a doctor who treats cancer). He was a very successful doctor and founded a clinic in his old neighborhood in Montevideo. He broke into Uruguay's political scene in 1990, when he became the mayor of Montevideo. Vázquez was the city's first mayor from the new Frente Amplio party. He also ran for president in 1994, but lost. Two years later he was the head of the FA, and in 2004 he became the nation's first president from that party. In Vázquez's personal life, he is an avid soccer fan. He is married and has four children.

**MILTON WYNANTS VÁZQUEZ** (b. 1971) Wynants was born in Paysandú, a western city lying along the Uruguay River's banks. Wynants is a racing bicyclist and has competed in the Olympic Summer Games four times, in 1996, 2000, 2004, and 2008. In 2000, in the Olympics in Sydney, Australia, Wynants won the silver medal in the men's cycling points race (a bicycle race around a track). This medal was Uruguay's first since the 1964 Olympics. Wynants has also won two bronze medals and one silver medal in the Pan American Games, which bring together athletes from all over North and South America.

**Sights to See**

**BEACHES** Uruguay is famous for its beautiful beaches. Its most renowned seaside resort is Punta del Este. In addition to its popular beaches, restaurants, and hotels, one of its attractions is Casapueblo. Uruguayan artist Carlos Páez Vilaró created this sprawling building as his home, but it has come to hold a museum and hotel and offers amazing views of the water. During the summer, it hosts music concerts. Punta del Diablo is less well known than Punta del Este but is also home to stunning natural scenery. This small fishing village is located on the Atlantic coast, about 100 miles (161 km) northeast of Punta del Este. Its sandy beaches are rarely crowded, and the region also offers birdwatching, deep-sea fishing, and the opportunity to see and learn about endangered sea turtles.

**COLONIA DEL SACRAMENTO** Located about 75 miles (121 km) west of Montevideo, this historic city dates back to 1680. It sits on the banks of the Río de la Plata, and its historic neighborhood (the Barrio Histórico) is a cultural and historical treasure. After wandering the old town's narrow, winding streets, visitors can climb to the top of its lighthouse, or *faro*, for a view of the town and the river. Colonia also holds a variety of museums, including several related to the town's history.

**ESTANCIAS** For visitors who are tired of Uruguay's cities, a stay on an estancia is the perfect getaway. Ranches throughout the nation's countryside offer guests a taste of rural life. Horseback riding, campfires, and hikes are a few of the attractions. For travelers who stay at estancias in the northern part of the country, the gaucho town of Tacuarembó is not far away. It hosts an annual gaucho festival and also has a museum of gaucho culture and history.

**ISLA DE LOBOS** This precious wildlife reserve is home to seals and sea lions. In fact, it houses one of the largest colonies of sea lions in the world, with more than 150,000 of the creatures. Boat tours bring nature lovers to the island to see the animals, and the island also has a wide variety of native vegetation.

**MONTEVIDEO** Uruguay's capital and largest city, Montevideo offers visitors a wide variety of sights and attractions. Stately government buildings, impressive Catholic cathedrals, historic monuments, and modern skyscrapers all mingle in this bustling center. The city's main square, Plaza Independencia (Independence Square), is a pleasant place to stroll and also features the tomb of José Artigas. The city is home to many museums, which present collections of art, crafts, and historical artifacts. There's also plenty of dining and shopping. For example, the large Mercado del Puerto (Port Market) bustles with vendors selling crafts and other goods, and the site also offers places to eat.

**colony:** a territory ruled and occupied by a foreign power

**dictator:** a leader who rules with complete control, often through the use of violence or other harsh methods

**estuary:** a body of water where fresh and salt waters mingle. Estuaries occur when rivers meet the ocean. The Río de la Plata is an estuary.

**gaucho:** a South American cowboy. Uruguay and Argentina were both once home to many gauchos who herded cattle across the region's open plains.

**gross domestic product (GDP):** a measure of the total value of goods and services produced within a country's boundaries in a certain amount of time (usually one year), regardless of the citizenship of the producers

**immigrant:** someone who arrives to live in a new country

**indigenous:** native to a particular place

**inflation:** rapidly rising prices, usually paired with a decrease in the value of a nation's currency

**Latin America:** Mexico, Central America, South America, and the islands of the West Indies. Latin America includes thirty-three independent countries, including Uruguay.

**literacy:** the ability to read and write a basic sentence. A country's literacy rate is one indicator of its level of human development.

**missionary:** a religious person who works in a foreign country. Missionaries often attempt to convert people to their religion, but they may also build hospitals, establish schools, and do other community work.

**yerba maté:** a tealike beverage made from the leaves of a South American shrub in the holly family. Yerba maté, often simply called maté, is very popular in Uruguay.

Glossary

Box, Ben. *South American Handbook*. Bath, England: Footprint, 2008.
This travel guide covers Uruguay and its fellow South American nations and includes historical, cultural, and geographical information.

*Europa World Yearbook, 2008*. Vol. 2. London: Europa Publications, 2008.
Covering Uruguay's recent history, economy, and government, this annual publication also provides a wealth of statistics on population, employment, trade, and more.

*The International Year Book and Statesmen's Who's Who*. London: Burke's Peerage Ltd., 2007.
This annual publication provides information on Uruguay's economy, politics, people, and more.

*Latin America*. Washington, D.C.: Stryker-Post Publications, 2008.
Released yearly, this resource presents articles about the history and culture of Latin American nations.

New York Times Company. *The New York Times on the Web*. 2008.
http://www.nytimes.com (February 10, 2009).
This on-line version of the newspaper offers current news stories along with an archive of articles on Uruguay.

"PRB 2008 World Population Data Sheet." *Population Reference Bureau (PRB)*. 2008.
http://www.prb.org (January 10, 2009).
This annual statistics sheet provides a wealth of data on Uruguay's population, birth and death rates, fertility rate, infant mortality rate, and other useful demographic information.

Turner, Barry, ed. *The Statesman's Yearbook: The Politics, Cultures, and Economies of the World, 2009*. New York: Macmillan Press, 2008.
This resource provides concise information on Uruguay's history, climate, government, economy, and culture, including relevant statistics.

UNDP. "Uruguay: 2008 Statistical Update." *Human Development Reports*. 2008.
http://hdrstats.undp.org/2008/countries/country_fact_sheets/cty_fs_URY.html (March 3, 2009).
The website, published by the United Nations Development Program (UNDP), presents a range of statistics on Uruguayan life. Information is available on health, education, the environment, and more.

UNICEF. "At a Glance: Uruguay." *UNICEF: Information by Country*. 2009.
http://www.unicef.org/infobycountry/uruguay.html (March 3, 2009).
This site from the United Nations agency UNICEF offers details about education, nutrition, and other demographics in Uruguay.

**U.S. Department of State. "Uruguay: Country Reports on Human Rights Practices—2007."** *U.S. Department of State: Country Reports on Human Rights Practices.* **2008.**
http://www.state.gov/g/drl/rls/hrrpt/2007/100656.htm (March 3, 2009).

This website is published by the U.S. State Department's Bureau of Democracy, Human Rights, and Labor. It provides a yearly update on the human rights situation within Uruguay, including concerns about women's rights, treatment of ethnic minorities, and other issues.

**World Health Organization. "Uruguay."** *World Health Organization: Countries.* **2009.**
http://www.who.int/countries/ury/en/ (March 3, 2009).

This website provides a wealth of statistics and information on health issues in Uruguay.

*BBC News—Americas*
http://news.bbc.co.uk/2/hi/americas/default.stm
This news site provides a range of up-to-date information and archived articles about Uruguay and the surrounding region.

*Candombe.com*
http://www.candombe.com/english.html
Visit this site to learn more about the history and culture of Uruguay's candombe music and to hear clips of candombe performances.

*CNN.com International*
http://edition.cnn.com/WORLD/
Check CNN for current events and breaking news about Uruguay, as well as a searchable archive of older articles.

**Draper, Allison Stark.** *Hydropower of the Future: New Ways of Turning Water into Energy.* **New York: Rosen Publishing Group, 2003.**
Most of Uruguay's energy comes from hydropower. This book examines this way of producing power.

*Embassy of Uruguay in the United States of America*
http://www.uruwashi.org/
Learn more about Uruguayan people, culture, and politics from this official embassy website.

*FIFA.com—Uruguay*
http://www.fifa.com/associations/association=uru/index.html
Futbol fanatics can check on Uruguay's statistics, players, and more at this site.

*Lonely Planet: Uruguay*
http://www.lonelyplanet.com/uruguay
Visit this website for information about traveling to Uruguay, as well as background information about the country.

*National Geographic: Giant Anteater*
http://animals.nationalgeographic.com/animals/mammals/giant-anteater.html
This site presents facts about the giant anteater, as well as a photo and even a recording of an anteater's call.

**Parnell, Helga.** *Cooking the South American Way.* **Minneapolis: Lerner Publishing Company, 2003.**
This cookbook presents a selection of recipes from Uruguay and its surrounding region. Cooks in Uruguay and throughout South America use many of the same ingredients and methods to prepare meals.

**Streissguth, Tom.** *Argentina in Pictures.* **Minneapolis: Twenty-First Century Books, 2003.**
As Uruguay's neighbor to the southwest and as another former Spanish colony, Argentina shares many cultural and historical ties with Uruguay. Read this book to learn more about this nation.

**Streissguth, Tom.** *Brazil in Pictures.* **Minneapolis: Twenty-First Century Books, 2003.**
Like many other nations in South America, Brazil has historical, economic, and cultural ties to Uruguay. Learn more about Uruguay's northern neighbor in this book.

*vgsbooks.com*
http://www.vgsbooks.com
Visit vgsbooks.com, the homepage of the Visual Geography Series®. You can get linked to all sorts of useful on-line information, including geographical, historical, demographic, cultural, and economic websites. The vgsbooks.com site is a great resource for late-breaking news and statistics.

**Whelan, Gloria.** *The Disappeared.* **New York: Dial Books, 2008.**
This novel for young adults explores the fates and experiences of the "disappeared" in Argentina during the 1970s and 1980s. Although this story focuses on an Argentine family, the stories of Uruguayan victims are similar.

**Captions for photos appearing on cover and chapter openers:**

Cover: Colorful houses line a street in the capital city of Montevideo.

pp. 4–5 Wide areas of rolling pastures have helped to make Uruguay a prosperous agricultural country.

pp. 8–9 A river winds through Uruguay's coastal plain region.

pp. 18-19 The historic quarter of Colonia del Sacramento, originally founded in 1680, has cobblestone streets and old buildings.

pp. 38–39 Young Uruguayans perform a folk dance in Montevideo.

pp. 46–47 A *comparsa*, or Carnival band, plays candombe music. This comparsa is part of a *llamadas* parade during Carnival celebrations. The llamadas tradition began among slaves during colonial times.

pp. 52–53 A herd of cows enters a corral.

## Photo Acknowledgments

The images in this book are used with the permission of: © Domino/Lifesize/Getty Images, pp. 4–5, 8–9, 12, 14, 60; © XNR Productions, pp. 6, 10; © age fotostock/SuperStock, p. 15; © Stefan Boness/Panos Pictures, pp. 16–17, 18, 56 (both), 62; © Domino/The Image Bank/Getty Images, p. 19; © Jerry Ginsberg/DanitaDelimont.com, pp. 20–21; © British Library/HIP/The Image Works, p. 23; The Art Archive/Museo Historico Nacional Buenos Aires/Gianni Dagli Orti, pp. 25, 28; Mary Evans Picture Library/Everett Collection, p. 29; © MIGUEL ROJO/AFP/Getty Images, pp. 32, 42, 48; © Gregg Newton/CORBIS, p. 34; AP Photo/Marcelo Hernandez, p. 36; © Margie Politzer/Lonely Planet Images, pp. 38–39; © Win Initiative/Lifesize/Getty Images, p. 40 (left); © Iván Franco/epa/CORBIS, p. 40 (right); © Corey Wise/DanitaDelimont.com, p. 43; REUTERS/Andres Stapff, pp. 44, 46–47, 52–53; © Win Initiative/Taxi/Getty Images, p. 45; © Win Initiative/The Image Bank/Getty Images, p. 49; © Per Karlsson/DanitaDelimont.com, p. 51; © JUNG YEON-JE/AFP/Getty Images, p. 54; © Win Initiative/Photodisc/Getty Images, pp. 58–59; © Jason Laure/DanitaDelimont.com, p. 63; © Domino/Stone/Getty Images, p. 64; Image courtesy of Banknotes.com - Audrius Tomonis, p. 68; © Laura Westlund/Independent Picture Service, p. 69.

Front cover: © Philip Coblentz/Brand X Pictures/Photolibrary.

Back cover: NASA.